The FUNOMENAL™ WORKPLACE

Energizing People & Culture
with the Positive Power of Fun

(YES, this works at home too!)

From the Former Ambassador of FUN for Southwest Airlines
One of the 1st to Pioneer the Positivity Movement in Corporate America

T O N Y   B R I G M O N

Disclaimer

This book is not affiliated or endorsed by Southwest Airlines in any way, and the author, Tony Brigmon, explicitly makes no such express claims. The author is a former employee and "Ambassador of Fun" for Southwest Airlines and writes from his personal perspective.

Contents

Acknowledgements

To Charlotte, my eternal companion, and the best teacher I've ever seen -- a tireless example of how to keep on keeping on, no matter what, until the job is done right.

To our awesome six children -- Rachael, Nathan, Briana, Blake, Elizabeth and Luke -- and delightful grandchildren. May you continue to face every difficulty courageously and endure to the end successfully.

To Howard Putnam, former CEO of Southwest Airlines, who took a BIG risk by letting me represent Southwest Airlines in the beginning as their Goodwill Ambassador and later as their official Ambassador of Fun, launching a speaking career that has given me more satisfaction than you can possibly imagine.

To Koby Fleck, for putting positive pressure on me to finish this book by pre-selling 110 copies. For this and a plethora of other FUNtastic things, thank you, Koby. And to his wife Jamie for coming up with the title of the book. Wow. You are indeed funomenal, Jamie. Thank you.

To Greg Clock (ClockWriting.com), for his offer of an "extra set of eyes" to clean up what I messed up with grammar and spelling. And to Nicole Hopkins and Braylyn Yancy for their assistance as well.

To Robin Ghio, for taking a break from his Employment and Immigration law practice to come up for air to add his vintage Ghio humor to the text on the book cover. Thank you, my friend.

To each and every one of you who cannot be named because it would double the length of this book. If you have ever made me smile, laugh out loud, or helped me in any way, I'm talking about YOU. You know who you are. Getting to interact with, learn from, and share fun stuff with ALL of you has made my life FUNtastic indeed. Thank you.

Testimonials

"The Best Way to Do Your Work and Succeed"
"For too long, many of us in business have thought fun was something you have after you do your work. In this book, Tony teaches us that fun is the best way to do your work and succeed." - Jim Stovall, Bestselling Author, *The Ultimate Gift* (now a 20th Century Fox major motion picture)

"Tony has a gift for looking at life in a fun way and capturing life lessons in a manner that sticks"
"Tony Brigmon was our 'Ambassador of FUN' when I was CEO. Tony has a gift for looking at life in a fun way and capturing life lessons in a manner that 'sticks' – making them easy to recall and use." - Howard Putnam, Former CEO, Southwest Airlines, Speaker, Author

"Tony creates a positive, supportive and encouraging 'zone' around him."
"I've seen Tony interact with people as a speaker, as a member of a group, and on an individual coaching basis. In all of these environments, Tony creates a positive, supportive, and encouraging 'zone' around him. Once you enter that zone, you know that three things are going to happen.

"First, you are going to have fun. Second, you are going to see things in a new and more positive way. And third, you are going to walk away feeling a whole lot better about who you are and what you can accomplish." - Rob Ghio, Law Office of Rob Ghio, P.C.

"... Tony Brigmon's program, by far, has been the most talked about and remembered!"
"I have brought in speakers from Dr. Steven Covey to Dr. Bob Arnot from CBS News, and Tony Brigmon's program, by far, has been the most talked about and remembered!" - Robin G. Williams, St. Luke's Hospital, Houston, Texas

"...none have left me with such a sense of uplift, happiness, and everything is going to be 'great' as Tony Brigmon."

"I have heard many 'motivational' speakers during the past 36 years of serving as Executive Director of SME, but none have left me with such a sense of uplift, happiness, and everything is going to be 'great' as Tony Brigmon." - Lew Butterfield, Sales & Marketing Association, Los Angeles, California

"... the underlying messaging of sound principles that put him in a class above other presenters on the professional speaking circuit."

"Tony's delivery was both captivating and on target in reinforcing key themes of our Customer Service program launch. His humor, timing, and delivery put him on par with the very best of entertainers, but it is the underlying messaging of sound principles that put him in a class above other presenters on the professional speaking circuit." - Martin Babinec, CEO/Founder, TriNet Group, San Leandro, California

"It was as if he had worked in our industry all his life because he knew of our particular challenges and used his material to solve/address them."

"What we got in Tony was a fun, professional speaker that had the group literally on the edge of their seats for the entire program. It was as if he had worked in our industry all his life because he knew of our particular challenges and used his material to solve/address them.

"The best way to tell how much impact a speaker has on a conference is to listen to the 'buzz' after. The feedback we received was all positive. They enjoyed his style, his humor, and his engaging methods of keeping us involved in his presentation." - Douglas Fry, Southeastern Advertising Publishers Association (SAPA), Columbia, Tennessee

Introduction

FUNomenal™ is pronounced the same as phenomenal. Google defines phenomenal as "very remarkable; extraordinary."

I define FUNomenal™ as `"WAY better than phenomenal; funtastic; funtabulous; best of the best.`` Now, you know. You can be FUNomenal™, too!

One morning, I woke up in Seabrook, Texas, a quaint town near NASA, in the Houston area. I had just delivered the keynote address for the Neighbors Emergency Center 2ᴺᵈ Annual Investor Conference the day before and was preparing to head home.

As I wrote my daily *"What would be GREAT today?"* list, my first thought was that it would be great "if I had a safe, timely, and fun flight back to Dallas."

To my delight, the flight WAS safe. It WAS timely. It WAS fun. (We even arrived 10 minutes early. Go Southwest Airlines!)

On the flight, I sat next to a man named Roy. This is where the fun comes in. He and his brother are the co-founders of Beanfields foods. (Yes, it was really him. His picture is on the back of the chip package.)

Roy and his marketing team were headed to Dallas for the Kroger Trade Show to launch a new product, their Bean & Rice Chips Nacho product, to be carried in Kroger stores.

During the flight, Roy and I had a fun conversation. As we were taxiing to the gate, he reached into his bag and pulled out the only Beanfields sample he had left on him and gave it to me.

I thanked him and said, "Roy, if I opened these Nachos right now and ate every one of them, and didn't share ANY with my wife Charlotte, could we keep this our little secret?"

Roy said, "Aw man, you gotta share the love!" I said, "So, you're gonna play the guilt card on me, huh?"

He said, "No, it's not that. It's just that it's the woman who usually buys the groceries." Ha-ha. Brilliant!

As soon as I reached my car in the airport parking lot, I drove straight to the Early Voting location near Joe Pool Lake in Grand Prairie, Texas. My wife, Charlotte, is the lead clerk there. I was so excited to "share the love" with her and her three coworkers - to their delight (an unexpected gift at an unexpected time).

Roy was right. You gotta share the love. And I believe I am right in making this prediction: Roy and his family will continually prosper with their "You gotta share the love" marketing philosophy.

Needless to say, last night, one of the three things on my *"What WAS GREAT Today?"* list was, yep, "I had a safe, timely, and fun flight to Dallas! For which I am grateful."

I suppose my "Serious fun -- Serious results" philosophy began my senior year in high school with an incident that happened with my English teacher, Mrs. Wear. She was long on homework assignments and short on patience with A.D.D. guys like me.

But a fun comment, at the right time and in the right way, taught me a memorable lesson on the power of fun to get serious positive results. I began to view fun in a totally different way after that.

Here's what happened.

I got elbowed in the eye in basketball practice. When I showed up in class the next day with a shiner, Mrs. Wear asked me what happened. That fun feeling that had so often gotten me into trouble came over me and I said in a deadpan way, "It's embarrassing Mrs. Wear. I don't want to talk about it."

This only flamed the fire of her curiosity and she insisted in a firm voice, "I really want to know."

And then a hush fell over the class in anticipation of my answer. I said, "I got into a fight with a guy who said you weren't the prettiest teacher in school." Audible groans could be heard all over the room.

To my shock, instead of getting angry with me, Mrs. Wear smiled and said, "Mr. Brigmon, you are exempt from this evening's homework assignment." This elicited a protest from one of the boys in class who blurted out, "He didn't get in a fight!"

Mrs. Wear was on him like a chicken on a June bug saying, "I'm aware of that. He still gets a pass on the homework assignment. You have a problem with that?" He didn't. And neither did I.

Yes indeed, at the right time and when used in the right way, real fun can get you real results that will make your day. Thank you, Mrs. Wear, for all you taught me.

If Mrs. Wear could see this book today her reaction would no doubt be, "Tony Brigmon wrote a book? I never knew he'd even read a book."

I was meeting with a client and a couple of his associates about special messages he'd like for me to deliver in an upcoming keynote for a conference. Near the end of the meeting as I was describing the power of fun to bring out the best in everyone he said, "I don't think anyone around here would describe me as a 'fun' person. I'm a very serious person."

I said, "I have evidence to the contrary." He looked startled and said, "What do you mean?" I said, "When I first arrived, I heard you speaking with someone about an upcoming trip with your family that you were really looking forward to.

"Talking about what you're looking forward to puts your brain in a state of positive -- which is how I define 'fun.'

"Then you listened to your associate describe something he was looking forward to. This allowed him to have 'fun' too.

"Then just before our meeting started, you made sure each of us had our beverage of choice to enjoy during the meeting. Another 'fun' thing for you to do, and for us to enjoy.

"Then after the meeting started, and I was sharing what I do, you listened attentively without interrupting. Since I love to share fun things, you made it easy for me to do this.

"And lastly, you described something that you were planning to do for those who work for you -- to ensure they know someone cares about them.

"Sir, if you add up all of these 'fun', selfless things you've done since I arrived -- you may be the most 'fun' person in the room.

"Yes, you are a serious person. Serious about 'fun.' Keep this up and you will continue to get serious results -- to the delight of everyone."

This is indeed "FUN." You get more DONE. And this makes you FUNOMENAL™.

The stories that follow are examples of many great teachers and FUNtastic experiences (over three decades) with people who "shared the love" of great life lessons with me -- whether they realized it or not. Now, I pass these on to you in the same "share the love" spirit.

Look for the following in each story:
1. Point
2. Fun reminder: Breathe in; Breathe out; Smile
3. FUNOMENAL™ Positivity Best Practice
4. Invitation to action
5. Good Note to Self
6. Smile and Wave graphic reminder to live a FUNOMENAL™ life every day, to bring out the best in everyone, everywhere – inspiring more FUN and productivity.

According to Harvard research, your brain at positive is 31% more productive than your brain is at negative, neutral, or stressed.

You're 37% better at sales. Doctors are 19% faster and more accurate at coming up with the correct diagnosis when positive instead of negative, neutral, or stressed.

Each story will help you see yourself doing positive things. As I always say, "What you see yourself doing over time, you will find yourself doing at the right time."

Each best practice has both a professional and a personal application. Because, hey, you gotta have a life outside of work, right? Right.

And some of the FUNOMENAL™ Positivity Best Practices are really fun. I'll share one with you here.

Recently I read that a 20-second hug from someone you know and trust reduces the harmful physical effects of stress, including its impact on your blood pressure and heart rate.

So, just for fun one morning, I asked my wife if she would do the 20-second hug experiment with me -- to put this feel-good research to the test.

I said, "Let's do one 20-second hug now and another one tonight." She smiled and agreed. WOW. I never realized research could be so much fun.

After the second 20-second hug that evening she said, "You shorted me 4 seconds on that hug." We both laughed. I promised her it would never happen again.

I highly recommend this fun best practice with loved ones to reduce stress and boost happiness.

Lastly, at the end of each story, just before the transition to the next story, I sum it up with a Good Note to Self. Here is an example of one I use in my Change Management presentation.

"It is what it is till it ain't. That they would if they could but they can't. Till they can. Then they will. And that's the deal. Deal with it." – Tony Brigmon

You will also notice I end every story with this fun visual reminder:

Smile & Wave
Make someone's day!

Why? Because it's FUN! And the positive energy of FUN helps you get more DONE.

A smile and friendly wave gets you a better return than a frown and unfriendly stare. That's because a smile and wave boosts happiness in both the giver and receiver.

And speaking of getting more DONE, here's a researched-proven best practice to help you do just that.

"Saying the word DONE can help you get more accomplished on your to-do list. Telling ourselves that we're done creates not only an emotional reaction but a physiological response as well," says Leslie Sherlin, a psychologist, neuroperformance specialist, and the co-founder of the brain-training company SenseLabs.

"The more often you complete a task, the more confidence you build to achieve the next item on your to-do list, allowing you to take on even more challenging tasks -- and set yourself up for increasing productivity."

Smile and wave. Make someone's day. Have more FUN. Get more DONE. This is the FUNOMENAL™ life!

This will inspire others to want to "get a life" too -- a FUN life -- and be FUNOMENAL™ like YOU. You can do this. YNOT today?

And speaking of FUN, to help improve your recall of the **FUNOMENAL™ Positivity Best Practices** (which are found in the "Serious Fun -- Serious Results" section of this book), I have placed the **FUNOMENAL™ Nuggets of Positivity (at a glance)** list for your review before the **"S.M.I.L.E. Positivity Best Practices."**

The **"S.M.I.L.E. Positivity Best Practices"** and the **"Good Notes to Self" Workbook** at the end of the book -- are proven positivity boosters. I invite you to discover what they can do for you.

Apply the FUNOMENAL™ Positivity Best Practices in the following pages and the results will be FUNtastic. Really.

*** Spoiler Alert: the **MAIN THANG** is at The End. Don't miss it!

Did I mention that all of the FUNOMENAL™ Positivity Best Practices in the stories have a workplace and a home place application? Okay I did, but I'll do it again: they do.

Are you ready for a Funomenal™ "Serious Fun - Serious Results" experience? Let's get started.

Discover and Prosper with Your Unique Ability

Everyone has a unique ability that can be used to serve others. One of our employees at Southwest Airlines became legendary for using hers. I'll call her Carol. Because that's her name.

Carol could walk into a riot and have everyone laughing within moments and chilling out. One night while she was working at the gate, a BIG guy, thinking he was late for his flight, and wasn't, came rushing up to her and said, "Do I have time to go to the restroom?"

She said, "I don't know. I've never timed you?" He laughed and went to the restroom. When he returned, the first words out of Carol's mouth were, "Sir, that took you three minutes. If you ever need to know, you're a three-minute bathroom person!" He laughed and boarded his flight. Do you think he'll ever forget Carol? Not a chance.

Carol could get away with this because it was her unique ability. You have one as well.

The stories and "Good Notes to Self" I'll be sharing with you will help you MAXIMIZE your unique ability. They are all about lessons I've learned from great teachers, some at Southwest Airlines. Some of my greatest lessons came from experiences I had while delivering over 2000 keynote presentations to some of the country's top organizations. I've had very good teachers in all of these environments.

Some of my teachers taught me how to talk so people would listen, others how to listen so people would talk. Some taught me how to problem-solve so both sides win. Others taught me how to use the power of music for personal development and professional success. And a few amazing teachers taught me how to be irresistibly attractive in communication, regardless of age or physical appearance.

I'll be sharing ALL of this and much MORE with you.

Now pause and breathe in ... breathe out, with a HINT of a smile. WOW. Looks GOOD on you. Y-E-A-H.

FUNOMENAL™ Positivity Best Practice: Here are two things you can do to discover your unique ability if you don't already know what it is. First, send an email to family and friends with this question: What do you see as my unique ability and how do you see me using it to serve others?

Second, think of a time when you were doing something that made you feel most alive. Think of ways you can do more of THAT now while serving others.

Do this for YOU. For self-renewal. For personal development. You deserve it.

When I did this my family and friends said, "Your unique ability is the way you share things. You're fun to listen to. You help us see things in new and more positive ways and feel better about who we are and what we can accomplish."

It's true. I LOVE sharing. The more I get to share, the more alive I become. So, I'll be VERY alive throughout the remainder of this book sharing my energize-engage-enrich stories and "Good Notes to Self" with you.

Be FUNOMENAL™: have more fun, get more done, and bring out the best in everyone. You can do this.

"Do what you do best, that makes you most alive. Serve enough others with it and you WILL thrive." - Tony Brigmon

Boost Your Happiness with a Calendar

There's a story told about Ken and Edna. Every year they'd go to the state fair and every year Ken would say, "Edna, I want to take that helicopter ride," and every year Edna would say, "Ken, I know. But that helicopter ride is 50 bucks and 50 bucks is 50 bucks!"

One year at the state fair, when they were 75 years old, a pilot overheard their exchange. As soon as he heard Edna say, "50 bucks is 50 bucks!" he said, "Folks, I'll tell you what. I'll take you both up for a ride. If you can stay quiet the entire time I won't charge you a penny. But if you say one word, it's 50 dollars."

They agreed and up they went. The pilot did all kinds of fancy maneuvers. Not a word. He went into his daredevil tricks over and over. Not a word was heard. When they landed the pilot said to Ken, "Well, buddy, I tell you what. I tried everything I could to get you to yell out and you didn't. I'm impressed."

Ken said, "Well, to tell you the truth I almost said something when Edna fell out. But you know, 50 bucks is 50 bucks!"

Sometimes, 50 bucks means more than 50 bucks. Sometimes, it's priceless when it means you get to do something that's important to you. It's motivating. It can stir excitement deep within you.

It can regenerate passion you thought you had lost due to the same old, same old routine of everyday life. It reminds you that you have unmet goals that still can be met.

Research shows that seeing something on your calendar that you're looking forward to will boost your happiness about as much as the actual experience will.

Now pause and breathe in ... Breathe out, with a HINT of a smile. WOW. Looks GOOD on you. Y-E-A-H.

FUNOMENAL™ Positivity Best Practice: What can you do today to turn a dream into a reality? Think of something you'd love to do and what doing it would do for you. Find out what it'd take to do it. Put it on your calendar and look at it frequently.

The journey of a thousand miles begins and ends with, yep, one step. But now, there's only ONE thing to do: The next one thing toward what you're looking forward to. Do it TODAY.

If you take the next step TODAY toward something you'd love to do, and put it on your calendar, you'll have something to look forward to. And you'll feel something delightful inside of you. It's called happiness. And others will feel it and like it too.

"If you don't do what you look forward to, you'll have something to look back on that you won't look forward to. Do it." - Tony Brigmon

How to Turn Irate People into Your Biggest Fans

Before becoming Southwest Airlines' Ambassador of FUN, I worked in the reservations department. One day, I got a call from a lady requesting a seat on a reduced rate flight.

I checked and said, "Ma'am I'm sorry, the flight is full. Can I check another time for you?" She said, "No, I want on THAT flight. Do you know who you're talking to?"

I said, "No ma'am." She said, "You're talking to Mrs. So and So and So and So, the 3rd. And just who am I talking to?" When she asked that question I knew two things. One, she did NOT know my name. And second, I knew her attitude was TICKING me off.

I said, "Ma'am, the question is not who you ARE talking to. It's who you WERE talking to!" And I hung up.

What did she do? Yep. She called back and asked for the manager and reported me. Lucky for me the manager liked me and gave me a chance to make it right.

I had to call her back, apologize and listen to her chew me out again.

Did she have some fascinating things to say to me on that call? Yes, indeed! And I knew, if I was gonna survive at Southwest Airlines, I'd have to do something different.

Then I remembered something I had learned while working in a mental health center in college. You should never interrupt an insane person while they're venting. If you did, they would flip out and become incredibly strong.

So I posted a little humorous reminder sign on my cubicle that read, "People who ask you, 'Do you know who you're talking to?' They are INSANE. Listen!"

The next time I got a call from an irate person, I imagined they were insane and I smiled and listened to all they had to say until there was nothing left to say. And then everything changed for the better for me and for them.

And so it is. Until people have been heard, they're not interested in your words. Listen until they hit bottom and have nothing more to say. Then there's only one direction to go. Up. They feel heard. They appreciate it. They become more cooperative. More receptive. They write letters of commendation.

My humorous "Listen!" sign helped me remember to listen with a smile.

I received so much positive feedback within a few months that I was promoted to a supervisor position. How about that?

Now pause and breathe in ... Breathe out, with a HINT of a smile. WOW. Looks GOOD on you. Y-E-A-H.

FUNOMENAL™ Positivity Best Practice: The next time you're talking to someone who's upset, simply listen to everything they have to say.

Tell them what you CAN do and WILL do to help them. And then do it. I invite you to do this at the next opportunity. Like TODAY.

"The most powerful 2-seconds? The pause after listening to ALL someone says before replying. It's their proof they've been heard." - Tony Brigmon

How to Open the Way to Anyone's Heart

I'm told one of the most amazing examples of our Southwest Airlines outrageous customer service stories took place at the old Sky Harbor Airport in Phoenix, Arizona.

At the edge of the airport was an animal control center. The ramp supervisor, a great dog lover, would stop by every day before work to see and admire the dogs.

One day, while one of his ramp agents was unloading a kennel with a sleeping German Shepherd in it from an arriving flight, he discovered that the dog was not sleeping. To his shock, he realized the dog was dead, and he immediately notified the supervisor.

It was a black German Shepherd.

Horrified, the supervisor said, "We can't deliver this dead dog to its owner." The ramp agent said, "What do you mean, the dog's dead. What else can you do?"

The supervisor said, "I'll tell you what we can do. I saw a black German Shepherd just like this one at the pound this morning. You drive over there and get it. We're gonna switch 'em. The agent said, "You've got to be kidding."

The supervisor said, "No, take the dead dog out. Put the collar on the live one. And I'll personally deliver it." The supervisor notified the owner, an elderly lady, that there would be a delay.

They got the dog and made the switch. Then the supervisor delivered the live dog and said, "Sorry for the delay, ma'am. Here's your dog."

She immediately said, "That's not MY dog." The supervisor said, "How do you know?" She said, "My dog's dead! He died on the trip and I'm bringing him home to bury him in my backyard. I want my dead dog."

The supervisor then confessed what they had tried to do and why, and the lady was impressed. They switched the dogs back and expressed their condolences.

But imagine her surprise when Southwest Airlines arranged for six ramp agents to show up with a new dog casket and serve as pallbearers and conduct a memorial service in her backyard.

And so it is, sometimes you can't bring a dead dog back to life, or even swap it with a live one to fool the owner.

But what you CAN do is to find creative ways to let someone know you care about them. The way to anyone's heart is an unexpected gift at an unexpected time.

Now pause and breathe in ... Breathe out, with a HINT of a smile. WOW. Looks GOOD on you. Y-E-A-H.

FUNOMENAL™ Positivity Best Practice: Think about what you can do TODAY to give an unexpected gift at an unexpected time. When someone shows up with a problem, do everything in your power to help them with it and then do something extra they're not expecting. Doesn't have to be outrageous, just thoughtful, caring and unexpected.

"An unexpected gift at an unexpected time is a delightful key that opens every door, but only every time." - Tony Brigmon

Boost Happiness with a Smile, Not a Grin

One day, Herb Kelleher, Co-founder of Southwest Airlines, asked me to participate in a brainstorming session about a concern he had with some new employees.

He invited ME to be part of the session because he said he needed some more craziness in the room -- BECAUSE craziness sparks creativity. I laughed and said, "Sure!"

The lady he hired to lead the session asked him a great opening question, "Herb, what do you want your new employees to do that they're not now doing?" He thought for a moment and said, "Smile! Some of these people look like they've been weaned on a pickle.

"And I want to walk over and ask them, 'Are you feeling all right?' But they'd get defensive and say, 'Yes, why do you ask?' Then I'd have to be honest and say, 'Well, when are you going to notify your face?' "

We all laughed and agreed that it's easier to hire a person that smiles than it is to train one to smile. But it CAN be done.

Obviously, you smile when you're happy. However, research shows the opposite is also true. Smiling actually makes you feel happier.

Without a smile, the expression on your face may be communicating messages about you that are simply NOT true. And what people see in your expression may give them a very wrong impression about you that can cost you dearly.

So it only makes sense to get in the habit of having a pleasant expression on your face at all times. And it can be done with practice.

Now pause and breathe in ... Breathe out, with a HINT of a smile. WOW. Looks GOOD on you. Y-E-A-H.

FUNOMENAL™ Positivity Best Practice: Let's practice right now. Put a smile on your face, not a grin. A grin is something people want to slap. What we're looking for is a smile or even a hint of a smile.

All right. Give it a go. Smile. Hold it for three seconds, or even better for three full breaths. Do it now. Wow. That does look good on you. Really.

A smile and a wave can make someone's day. And yours too.

If you share your smile TODAY, you'll be amazed at what it'll do for them and for you, your relationships, your creativity, and your productivity.

"Smile and wave. Make someone's day. You'll get rave reviews. Yea!" - Tony Brigmon

How to Cash in on Dumb Do's

There's a story told about Ken and Edna, an elderly couple, both country folks. One day when they had gotten really old, Edna said, "Ken, there's something I need to tell you. Something you need to know."

When she had his attention she continued, "Right after we got married I started keeping an emergency kit under the bed. And should something ever happen to me I just wanted you to know about it."

Ken said, "All right, Edna. Thanks for letting me know." Later on in the day, when Edna was out of the house, curiosity got the best of Ken and he went into the bedroom and looked under the bed. Sure enough, there it was: a box with a lid on it.

He pulled out the box, opened the lid and, to his shock, saw three eggs and a LOT of money. He counted it. It was over 60,000 dollars. Now his curiosity was on fire. When Edna returned, he confessed.

He said, "Edna, I shouldn't have done it, but I did. I looked in the emergency kit and I gotta ask you, "Why do you have three eggs in there?"

She said, "Well, right after we got married, every time you did something really, really DUMB, I'd put an egg in there." Ken smiled and thought to himself, "That's not too bad, over all these years, only three Dumb Do's? Not bad. Not bad at all."

Then he asked, "What about the 60,000 dollars?" She said, "Oh, every time I had a dozen in there, I'd sell 'em!"

The Truth is we've all committed a lot of Dumb Do's. But they only remain Dumb until we find a way to convert them into wisdom and even cash in on them like Edna did.

Some of the dumbest things I've ever done have taught me some of my most valuable lessons which that have served me well throughout my life.

Dumb Do's teach you what NOT to do. Often, if you'll just do the opposite next time, you'll find it's the smart thing to do and the right Do for you.

Now pause and breathe in ... Breathe out, with a HINT of a smile. WOW. Looks GOOD on you. Y-E-A-H.

FUNOMENAL™ Positivity Best Practice: Reflect on this question TODAY: What have my Dumb Do's taught me? Then write down all the responses that surface. What you'll have when you're done is your own custom Life Lessons list from your own life experiences of smart things to remember so you can cash in on them at the right time when the opportunity presents itself.

You can also learn from the Dumb Do's of others that you observe, read or hear about. Cash in on all Dumb Do's TODAY, with gratitude. It's a smart to thing to do.

Be FUNOMENAL™: have more fun, get more done, and bring out the best in everyone. You can do this.

"Don't repeat a Dumb Do. That's what Dumber would do. Be smart. Let the Do's teach you." - Tony Brigmon

Toss the Boss Out of Your Relationships

My wife is half Italian. I'm from Louisiana. When we combined our two strong personalities under the same roof, the question eventually arose, "Who's the boss?"

When we discussed this one day she said, "I'll tell you what. You can be the boss as long as I'm the decision maker." Sounded good to me. I'm still trying to figure out exactly what "boss" means.

Like most couples, we don't always see eye-to-eye on things. But when I'm willing to hear her out, more often than not I acquiesce. Because she's usually right.

One of my macho acquaintances saw this as a weakness in me as a "man" and chided me, "Hey, who wears the pants around your house? You better 'Man-up' and show her who's the boss."

One day, I was giving a presentation and I saw him in the audience. I couldn't resist saying, "Some of my friends question me about who wears the pants around my house.

"And they might be surprised to know that my wife recently came to me on her hands and knees. That's right. And they might be interested in knowing what she said to me while she was on her hands and knees.

"She said, 'Come out from under that bed you coward and fight like a man!' " Okay, the part about her coming to me on hands and knees did NOT happen.

What DID happen is I learned through many years of marriage it's best not to have bosses. It's better to have leaders. And whoever is best suited to lead in a given situation leads, with the other as a supportive follower.

"Who's right?" is not as important as "What's right?" And I am grateful to have a wife who always seeks to do the right thing and encourages me to do the same.

Actually, my wife's much better at details and doing research than I am. My strength is in spontaneous situations. We IS better than ME. And together everyone accomplishes more, no doubt.

What's the distinction between bosses and leaders? Leaders inspire motivated followers. That's because they lead from the front by example.

Leaders also understand followers WILL support what they help create. So they invite those they lead to be part of the creative process.

Some bosses think they're smarter than everyone else and exclude them from the decisions.

They alienate those they boss to the point they lose their respect. And then, the employees fire the boss through less productivity. And once they fire the boss, it's only a matter of time before the organization makes it official.

Now pause and breathe in ... Breathe out, with a HINT of a smile. WOW. Looks GOOD on you. Y-E-A-H.

FUNOMENAL™ Positivity Best Practice: So whether you're a leader or a follower at work or at home, I invite you TODAY to ensure that all decisions are team decisions when possible, so the team can pull together, not apart.

Fire the boss TODAY, especially in your personal relationships. Decide together who can LEAD best and let them lead. Leader or follower, everyone has an important part to play. Just make sure everyone gets the opportunity to contribute with what they do best.

If you do this, you'll find that your team, professionally or personally, will get great results.

"If you're leading and no one is following, you're not a leader, you're a loner. The one who CAN lead should lead. Follow." - Tony Brigmon

Become Irresistibly Attractive in Conversation

I had the privilege of meeting Mr. Rogers from Mr. Rogers' Neighborhood in the early 80's. We were eating in the same restaurant.

I couldn't resist the opportunity, so I hesitantly walked over to his booth and said, "Mr. Rogers?" Yes, it was an awkward moment. I mean what do you say? "Fred?" He was SO gracious. I told him how much I appreciated the positive impact his show had on our family, especially our six children.

He immediately asked me for their names and had me write them on a napkin, adding my wife's name and our address. He asked me questions about each one of my children. And then said sincerely, "They're lucky to have you as a dad."

I tried to re-focus the conversation on him, but he kept smoothly directing it back to me. Two weeks later each member of my family received a signed 8" by 10" photo of Fred, with our names at the top.

When Fred Rogers passed away, we felt we had lost a friend in the neighborhood.

That old saying is true, "They don't care how much you know until they know how much you care about them." Everyone has something they care about, and the quickest way to connect with them is to pay attention to what they talk about. It won't take you long to find it.

Mr. Rogers spotted mine within the first sentence when I said, "My wife and I have raised six children." Boom. He had it. I care about my wife and my children or I wouldn't have brought it up. And he was on it like a chicken on a June bug.

Now pause and breathe in ... Breathe out, with a HINT of a smile. WOW. Looks GOOD on you. Y-E-A-H.

FUNOMENAL™ Positivity Best Practice: What can we do today to connect better with others? TODAY, I invite you to find out what someone cares about. Ask them to share a couple of things they care about and why.

Focus on what they say so you can remember. Then surprise them with an unexpected gift at an unexpected time related to what they care about.

In your conversations with others, if you get in the habit of making it all about them and what they care about, and find unexpected ways to let them know you remember, they'll love it and they'll always remember irresistibly attractive you.

"What makes you irresistibly attractive to others is when you make it all about them, not you. Do it. You'll love the review." - Tony Brigmon

How to Boost Morale with Anyone Anywhere

There's a story told by a past chairman of the FDIC about Herb Kelleher, the co-founder of Southwest Airlines. A friend of his, a CEO, called him one day and said, "Herb, we've got an employee morale problem over here, and I can't figure out what the problem is for the life of me.

"I was wondering if you might drop by sometime, when you have a few minutes, and help me figure it out." Herb agreed to give it a shot and arranged a time for a visit. His friend greeted him in the lobby. Then, they got on an elevator with about five to six employees and rode up in silence.

When they stepped off the elevator, Herb turned to his friend and said, "I already know what the problem is." His friend said, "Really? What is it?" Herb said, "YOU. You ARE the problem."

His friend said, "What do you mean?" So Herb said, "We just rode up an elevator together in silence with five or six of your employees. You didn't greet any of them by name or speak with any one of them about what's important to them. You fix THAT and you'll fix your morale problem."

Mark Kay Ash, the founder of Mary Kay Cosmetics, is quoted as saying, "Everyone has an invisible sign around their neck that reads, 'Make me feel important.' "

When you find ways to make people feel important, you become important to them. They'll be energized by you and find ways to make you proud of them.

Now pause and breathe in ... Breathe out, with a HINT of a smile. WOW. Looks GOOD on you. Y-E-A-H.

FUNOMENAL™ Positivity Best Practice: Here are two things you can do TODAY to make people feel important.

1. Use their name when you speak with them. It's their favorite sound. When I meet someone and want to remember their name I simply say, "I want to remember your name. Writing it down helps me do that. Is that okay with you?"

And it ALWAYS is. Plus, they make sure I get the spelling right, which is a BIG deal to them.

2. Talk with them about what's important to them. It's almost always going to be family or hobbies. But what's REALLY important to them will come up in their conversations, so pay attention. Then, write it down and add it to their contact information, so you can remember.

If they mention an accomplishment of a family member, write down the name of that family member so you can ask about them later. They'll love it and appreciate you for remembering.

So, use their names. Talk with them about what's important to them. Do this TODAY. You'll boost morale wherever you go, and if you're a leader, your team will follow you and have your back wherever you lead.

Lead on.

"You get a better return with the boomerang of respect than with the hand grenade of disrespect. Make them feel important. Listen." - Tony Brigmon

Smile & Wave
Make someone's day!

How to Take Anyone from Sad to Glad

I was about to depart San Antonio on a Southwest Airlines flight when I noticed a 5-year-old unaccompanied minor, named Shanie, sitting in the window seat across the aisle from me. The first time I glanced over, she seemed to be doing okay.

But the next time I glanced over, tears were streaming down Shanie's cheeks. I started to lean over and ask her what was wrong, but a flight attendant beat me to it. She said, "Shanie, what's the matter?" Shanie said, "I miss my daddy," who she had just been visiting.

Immediately, the flight attendant said, "We'll just have to write your daddy a letter." Shanie said, "I can't write." The flight attendant said, "But I can. You can help me with the words. We'll do it just as soon as we get up in the air. I promise."

Sure enough, once we were airborne and the safety belt sign was off, here came the flight attendant, just as she promised, with a stamped postcard. She copied the dad's address off the unaccompanied minor's card and then said, "Shanie, how about we write 'Dear Daddy, I had a great time.' "

Shanie said, "Write that." And so the flight attendant did. Then she said, "How about we say, 'I love you, Daddy.' " Shanie said, "Oh, yes, please write that." She did and then had Shanie print her name at the bottom of the card. After that, the flight attendant promised she would see that it got mailed at the next stop.

Then the flight attendant said, "Shanie, I need your help. Do you think you could help me make sure everyone gets plenty of peanuts?" Shanie smiled and said, "Yes!" Shanie gave us more peanuts than she should have, which made us happy. Because peanuts are about all you're gonna get on a Southwest Airlines flight. But if that helps keep those fares low, so be it.

Shanie went from sad to glad in no time. She was laughing and giggling when people complimented her on her cheerful service. I heard one passenger say to her, "I bet you're gonna grow up to be a Southwest Airlines flight attendant." And who knows, maybe she will.

And so it is. When you help someone who is sad or down do something positive and helpful for others, like the flight attendant did for Shanie by helping her write her daddy a letter and then inviting her to serve us peanuts, sadness is transformed into gladness or happiness for everyone.

Now pause and breathe in ... Breathe out, with a HINT of a smile. WOW. Looks GOOD on you. Y-E-A-H.

FUNOMENAL™ Positivity Best Practice: I invite you to pay attention TODAY to those around you. If you notice someone who appears sad or down, show them you care. Find out what's wrong if you can. And then invite them to do something positive with you for someone else. It'll make everyone happier. Really.

"Invite someone who is down to help you lift someone else up. There's no downside to UP. Lift together. Feel GOOD together." - Tony Brigmon

Use the Power of Music for Personal and Professional Success

In 1979, I walked into a conference room at Southwest Airlines to help enliven a customer care/employee development class with the fun things I do. I saw a jam box on a table with a cassette in it.

Okay, you can Google "cassette" if you're not old enough to know what it is.

As employees from three cities who didn't know each other well were streaming into the room, I pushed the play button on the boom box and, to my delight and that of everyone else, on came a Big Band song called "In the Mood." I cranked it up.

To my surprise, these people suddenly started talking to one another. Within moments, the noise level had doubled. A few people even broke into some funky dance moves. The energy in the room began to go UP and the stress in the room began to come DOWN.

After the first trainer had finished his part of the class, he walked over to me and excitedly said, "What a receptive group we've got today."

And I thought, "Good Note to Self": Have lively music playing when people walk into and out of a meeting." Because on that day, I learned that powerful meetings can be fun with the help of the right music and songs.

We don't just hear the music. We experience it. Music is the universal language that connects everyone, regardless of race, language or background.

As I began to experiment with music and songs that impact people's emotional states in positive ways, I came up with five categories which you can use to organize your favorite songs to give you, well, a life, personally and professionally. And if you already have a life, the power of music can help make it even better.

Now pause and breathe in ... Breathe out, with a HINT of a smile. WOW. Looks GOOD on you. Y-E-A-H.

FUNOMENAL™ Positivity Best Practice: TODAY, I invite you to arrange to get a copy of some popular energizing music and play it at the beginning and end of your next meeting. And notice what you notice. The fun energy from lively songs is contagious.

Think of the word MUSIC as an acronym and you'll easily remember the 5 categories I recommend. **M**otivate songs. **U**nwind songs. **S**mile songs. **I** Love Ya songs. And last but not least, **C**ommunicate songs to connect better with others.

Also, TODAY, I invite you to begin making a list of your favorite songs. Because I'm about to show you how to use them in five amazing ways, to spark more energy, less stress, more smiles, better relationships, and more receptivity to your ideas. Really.

Be FUNOMENAL™: have more fun, get more done, and bring out the best in everyone. You can do this.

"You don't just hear music, you experience it. Use it to energize yourself and others -- for a better experience." - Tony Brigmon

Use Motivate Songs to Captivate Success

Leon Spinks, former heavyweight boxing champion, was explaining to a reporter how he used the song Rocky to help him prepare for his title fight with Muhammad Ali.

He said, "At the end of my work out every day, the song Rocky was played. I imagined the fight was over, and I would jump up and down, with my hands in the air, celebrating my win."

Spinks went on to explain that when the bell rang for the actual fight, he went blank on everything he was trained to do against Ali. He said, "Instincts took over and I just went with it, just like in a fight in an alley."

Turns out his instincts served him well. Leon Spinks shocked the world that Las Vegas night of February 15, 1978, when he beat The Greatest, Muhammad Ali, and won the world heavyweight title in only his eighth professional fight.

And so it is, just like Leon Spinks used the song Rocky as his Motivate song to preview the feeling of success in an "impossible" fight against Ali, you can use Motivate songs of your choice to capture the feeling of success for yourself or someone you're working with.

This successful feeling will prompt impressions that feel right and, when acted upon immediately, will lead to your success in either what you're attempting or to something new even better suited for you.

Now pause and breathe in ... Breathe out, with a HINT of a smile. WOW. Looks GOOD on you. Y-E-A-H.

FUNOMENAL™ Positivity Best Practice: TODAY, I invite you to select a favorite Motivate song. It could be the "Rocky Theme" by Bill Conti, "Eye of the Tiger" by Survivor, the "William Tell Overture", whatever song makes you feel motivated.

The musical characteristics for Motivate Songs are usually fast tempo and lots of bass tones, with the volume cranked up to the level where you feel the energy the best.

Each time you play the song, imagine how it would feel if you had just been successful, doing something that's important to you.

This feeling of success, enhanced by the energy of the song, will prompt impressions just like it did for Leon Spinks to follow his unpredictable street-fighting instincts rather than what his coaches had trained him to do.

If you act immediately TODAY on the impressions you receive while listening to your Motivate song, you'll not only achieve more success, you will have discovered the most effective way to access your own inner FUNOMENAL™ Positivity Best Practices for achieving success through the power of music.

"Use Motivate Songs to preview the thrill of victory and to get over the agony of defeat. They can spark ideas for success." - Tony Brigmon

Smile & Wave
Make someone's day!

Use Unwind Songs to Let Go of the Worst for the Best

At the end of one of my keynote presentations, when I first began my speaking career, Dr. Don Michel, Chairman of the Music Therapy Department of Texas Women's University, approached me.

He said, "How spontaneous are you?" I replied, "Pretty spontaneous." To which he said, "Good, I'd like to show you our music table at school. It's only six blocks away. But we need to go now because I want to test something."

As soon as we arrived, he rolled out a portable biofeedback machine and tested my stress level. The meter went next to the highest reading. He smiled and said, "We'll call that positive stress because you're all keyed up from the fun stuff we were doing."

While still attached to the machine, he had me lie down on the table. It had speakers built into the under part of the table so I would not only hear the music, but I would feel it vibrating through the table as well.

He then pressed the play button on a looped recording of the classical song, "Pachelbel's Canon in D." Soft volume, slow tempo, lots of treble composition.

Six and a half minutes into the song he said, "Don't get up, but look at the monitor." I was now at next to the lowest level of relaxation and felt like I'd had a two-hour nap ... in only six and one-half minutes, not the typical 15 to 20 minutes it would take to attain a relaxation response through meditation.

He said, "THAT is the POWER of music."

When I recommended "Pachelbel's Canon in D" to one of my neighbors, he said, "I don't happen to have a copy of that Taco Bell's Canon in D."

And so it is. Unwind songs can "soothe even the savage beast." When it comes to unwind songs, it is different strokes for different folks. But the good news is there are all kinds of unwind music you can use to relax and refresh.

Now pause and breathe in ... Breathe out, with a HINT of a smile. WOW. Looks GOOD on you. Y-E-A-H.

FUNOMENAL™ Positivity Best Practice: TODAY, I invite you to use the power of music to de-stress before you take that stress out on someone you love or even a pet. If you don't already have a favorite unwind song, try some classical music like "Pachelbel's Canon," or "Tranquility" by Hennie Bekker, "A Day Without Rain" by Enya, or a "Kenny G Instrumental," or whatever music relaxes you.

Many classical radio stations play soothing Road Rage music daily. The next time you hear one you like, check your watch and call them. Tell them what time you heard it, and they'll give you the name of the music. How about that?

Take a stress break TODAY with your favorite unwind song before stress breaks you or a relationship with someone you care about.

"Listen to Unwind Songs. They send a clear message to stress: So long. Be gone." - Tony Brigmon

Smile & Wave
Make someone's day!

Use Smile Songs to Get Over It or Through It

When I first heard Ray Stevens song "The Mississippi Squirrel", about a squirrel that got loose in the First Self-Righteous Church of Pascagoula, I did not just smile, I laughed out loud.

Then, I began sharing it with my audiences and they laughed and loved it too, especially the positive energy it brought into the room.

So I began looking around for other Smile songs and discovered that Nashville songwriters are masters at using humor to cope with stress.

Some of my favorite titles to share with my audiences are:

- "I'll be under the table when I get over you"; or
- "I bought the shoes that just walked out on me"; or
- "She broke my heart and stomped that sucker flat"; or
- "My best friend just ran away with my wife and I miss him";
- And one that always gets a great response is, "The oil is all in Texas but the dipsticks are in DC."

And so it is. Laughter is a powerful antidote to stress, pain, and conflict. Nothing works faster or more dependably to bring your mind and body back into balance than a good laugh. Humor lightens your burdens, inspires hopes, connects you to others, and keeps you grounded, focused, and alert.

And there's no more energizing way to access laughter than through great Smile songs.

Now pause and breathe in ... Breathe out, with a HINT of a smile. WOW. Looks GOOD on you. Y-E-A-H.

FUNOMENAL™ Positivity Best Practice: I invite you TODAY to go to YouTube and type "Mississippi Squirrel by Ray Stevens" into the search bar. Listen to the song as you watch the delightful video. It's sure to put a smile on your face or a laugh in your belly.

Create a Smile Songs playlist folder on your computer, iPhone, Android device or whatever you use. When you hear a song that makes you smile or laugh, add it to your folder.

And then on those days when you start taking yourself too seriously, or as they say in West Texas, "You feel like you've been rode hard and put away wet" because of stress, you can click your Smile Songs playlist and smile and laugh that stress away through the power of fun songs. Do it TODAY.

"Listen to Smile Songs. They energize your sense of humor and make your other senses smile too." - Tony Brigmon

How to Kindle and Rekindle Love

We all have high moods and low moods. When we're in high moods, we say and do high-mood things. When we're in low moods, we say and do low-mood things.

Low moods, when not handled well, can hurt relationships. So, when our children were little and it was MY mood that was the problem, I'd go out into my office or up in my room and I'd play my frisky songs.

Now don't get ahead of me on that. A " f-r-i-s-k-y" song is any song that kindles or rekindles love and causes you to want to be with that special someone in your life. For me, it's my wife.

My Frisky songs are songs like Lee Greenwood's "I Owe You;" or Lou Rawls' "Lady Love." If you want to see me go totally wild, play Gladys Knight and the Pips' "Midnight Train to Georgia."

When she gets to the part in the song where she says, "I'd rather live with him in his world than live without him in mine!," I'm thinking now there is a WOMAN! Oh, YEAH!

I used to imagine my children were listening outside the door while I was listening to my songs and then running to their mom, saying "Momma, he's up there listening to his frisky songs!" And then I imagined her responding, "Oh, no!"

What I do know for sure is my frisky, I Love Ya songs made me fun to be with and made me want to be with HER on my very best behavior. And they can do this for you and your special someone too.

My wife's favorite frisky song? The Righteous Brothers "Unchained Melody." When I saw how much she liked that song, I went out and got me a copy. And if she ever hides my copy, I've got me a backup copy. Oh, yeah.

And so it is. I Love Ya songs help you remember the good times and put you in the mood for more good ones. They can say things for you better than you can say them at the perfect time. Let them.

Now pause and breathe in ... Breathe out, with a HINT of a smile. WOW. Looks GOOD on you. Y-E-A-H.

FUNOMENAL™ Positivity Best Practice: TODAY, I invite you to listen to your favorite I Love Ya song before spending time with that special person in your life. Or, even better, listen to your favorite song together. And if you don't have one, get one. H-e-l-l-o.

It'll help you remember who's important in your life and to treat that special someone that way.

"I Love Ya Songs say 'I love you' better and never tire of saying it ever. Do we tire of hearing it? Never." - Tony Brigmon

Smile & Wave
Make someone's day!

Use Communicate Songs to Connect with People in the Best Possible Way

I was speaking with my wife about one of her favorite frisky songs, the Righteous Brothers "Unchained Melody," and I asked her, "What do you like about that song? What does it say to you? What's it all about?"

She replied, "It's about commitment, passion, and total love." Then I had an AHA moment. What she likes about that song is what she values in her life. She values commitment, passion, and total love. I KNOW this to be true.

Commitment: For her, it means to keep your promises or don't promise.

Passion: If you really mean it, really say it. If you don't really mean it, don't try to say it. It'll be void of passion or meaning.

Total love: That's what she values most and that's what I want to give her.

Acting on a hunch, I called one of my best friends, a tell-it-like-it-is attorney. I asked him to name a favorite song. He said, "Lean On Me."

I asked, "What's that song all about to you?" He said, "Loyalty, friendship, and how friends support each other."

And when I thought back on why he considered me to be his good friend, it became clear it was because he knows I'm loyal to him, and I do strive to support things he's interested in. He knows he can lean on me, and I know he has MY back when I need him.

And so it is. A Communicate song is simply a favorite song of someone else. Your task is to find out what it is and what it communicates to THEM, so you can discover what they value most to connect to them in the best possible way.

Now pause and breathe in ... Breathe out, with a HINT of a smile. WOW. Looks GOOD on you. Y-E-A-H.

FUNOMENAL™ Positivity Best Practice: TODAY, I invite you to find out what someone's Communicate Song is. Ask them, "What's one of your favorite songs? What does that song say to you? What's it all about?"

And listen closely to what they say. What they say next will reveal to you what they value most. It will give you an irresistible way to communicate and connect better with them.

What if they say, "Grandma Got Run Over by a Reindeer?" What does that tell you? It tells ME they enjoy humor. And I'd be sure to include more of that in our communications.

I might even send them a copy of the song after our conversation to show them what they like MATTERS to me. Or, if I heard another funny song, I might send it to them, saying, "I heard this crazy song and thought you'd enjoy it as well."

Let the Communicate Songs of others communicate to you what they value most so you can connect with them in the best possible way. Please don't accept or reject this until you try it. Do it TODAY.

Be FUNOMENAL™: have more fun, get more done, and bring out the best in everyone. You can do this.

"When you know what someone's favorite song says to them, you learn what they value. Ask them. Then, give it to them. Priceless." - Tony Brigmon

How to Have Just About Anything You Want

There's an old saying, "You can have just about anything you want in life by giving enough other people what they want." Turns out, our Southwest Airlines story proved this to be true.

When we started out, what WE wanted was to be the Low Fare, High Care airline and have a lot of fun, while working hard. To get what WE wanted, we had to find out what our passengers wanted. So we did a curious thing: We asked them. And they did a curious thing: They told us.

They wanted low fares, flights that left on time, and when they arrived at their destinations, guess what they wanted to arrive with them? That's right, their bags.

So we decided to give them what they wanted. We figured out how to lower our overhead and prices by flying one kind of plane: 737s, which meant we could give them what they wanted: low fares.

By benchmarking Indy 500 pit crews, we used stopwatches to learn how to turn a plane in 10 minutes: people off, bags off -- people on, bags on -- pushing away from the gate in a total time of 10 minutes, something the industry had told us was IMPOSSIBLE to do.

For the bags part, we just looked at what everyone else was doing and decided not to do that. The result? For five years in a row, Southwest Airlines won the Triple Crown award: Least Lost Bags, Least Complaints and Most On-Time of all the other airlines.

And based on the most recent data available in 2016 from the U.S. Department of Transportation, Southwest Airlines is the nation's largest carrier in terms of originating domestic passengers boarded. How about that?

And so it is, give enough people what they want, and you can have just about anything you want. Using this formula, we became THE

Low-Fare, High-Care airline, legendary for hard work, outrageous customer service, and a fun culture.

Now pause and breathe in ... Breathe out, with a HINT of a smile. WOW. Looks GOOD on you. Y-E-A-H.

FUNOMENAL™ Positivity Best Practice: What we did at Southwest Airlines can work for you too. TODAY, I invite you to review what it is you REALLY want. Team up with others that want that as well.

Next, find out what it is that those you serve want that they're not now getting. Ask them. They'll tell you. Then put your heads together and come up with a way to give them what they want better than anyone else. We did it. You can do it too. Start TODAY.

This principle works in personal relationships as well as professional ones. People love to share what they want. And they'll love it and reward you like they did us when you give it to them. Start giving them what they want TODAY.

"Use what you love to do to help enough others get what they want. Then, you'll have what you want: happiness and success." – Tony Brigmon

Smile
&
Wave
Make someone's day!

Get the Results You Want with Accountability

After a few years of my marriage to my half-Italian wife, I discovered to my shock there were now an additional 70 pounds of me that she was not LEGALLY married to.

That's right. Her cooking was irresistible. And my overeating was making me miserable.

So I heard about a program called Overeaters Anonymous, one of the successful 12 Step Programs. What I liked about the program was it did not have eating plans. You came up with your own. But what they DID have were sponsors, someone you chose to be accountable to with your eating plan.

The accountability questions were simple: What are your plans? Will you let me know? When's a good time? How did it go? That's it.

I arranged a time with my sponsor to leave a voicemail report on an answering machine -- which automatically eliminated two of the questions "Will you let me know?" and "When's a good time?"

So I only had to answer two questions on each call, "How did it go?" and "What are your plans?"

I would briefly leave a voicemail sharing how it went and my plans for the next day. And then I would call the next morning at the agreed-upon time and give my next report.

The results? I lost over 35 pounds in two months and eventually reached my goal. One 60-year-old lady's plan in our group was simply to take two swallows of water after each bite of food. She lost 265 pounds.

You can use the power of accountability too. There's something about accounting to someone you respect that gives you willingness and power to stick to your plan.

Especially when you choose someone to whom you wouldn't want to give a bad report. There was NO way I was gonna call my sponsor and report I had NOT done what I said I'd do.

It was okay to change the plan, and I frequently did for a variety of reasons. That was totally up to me. And I was able to stick to it, thanks to the power of accountability.

Now pause and breathe in ... Breathe out, with a HINT of a smile. WOW. Looks GOOD on you. Y-E-A-H.

FUNOMENAL™ Positivity Best Practice: I invite you TODAY to test these accountability questions with something you find difficult to do on your own: procrastination, overeating, exercise, whatever it is you need to do and are NOT currently doing.

Think of someone who'd be good for you to account to. Someone you respect and wouldn't want to give a bad report. Someone you can ask to help you.

Remember the accountability questions: What are your plans? Will you let me know? When's a good time? How did it go?

If it turns out you don't do what you say three times in a row, it's three strikes and you're out. It's time to find a new person to account to. Try these accountability questions out TODAY. See what they do for you.

Proven Productivity Questions: What are your plans? Will you let me know? When's a good time? How did it go? Repeat often." Tony Brigmon

Clarify Your Values Before You Lose Value

One day a friend said to me, "May I share something with you? It has helped me get clear about what I value most, so I can be sure to make time for it in my life?" I was immediately interested and said, "Please do."

He said, "Write down six things you most enjoy doing. But leave some space after each one." So, I did.

He said, "Now write down when you last did each one, at least the month if not the day, or, maybe even sadly enough, the year." So I did that.

He said, "Write down what it cost (if anything) to do each one of those." So I did.

He said, "Do you do it alone or with others? Put 'A' for alone and 'WO' for With Others, below each one."

He said, "If five of the six things you like to do are alone, let's talk about what's going on in your life. Or if all six are with others, what happens to you when you are alone?"

Great questions! He said, "Now, add Outdoors or Indoors? 'O' for outdoor, and 'I' for indoor." I did that.

He said, "One more, add Primarily Physical or Primarily Mental below each one, using the letters 'PP' or 'PM.' " So, I did.

He then had me review my list and asked, "How much balance do you have in your life? Do you HAVE a life? Are you making time to do the things that are important to you?" More great questions!

Finally, he said, "Now complete this sentence, 'I'm beginning to suspect ___.' " I replied, "I'm beginning to suspect I don't have balance."

He said, "Complete this one, 'It's becoming clear that ___.' " To which I said, "It's becoming clear that my family needs me more in their lives."

He said, "Final one, 'Something I really CAN and WILL do is ___.' " I responded, "Something I really CAN and WILL do is to calendar more time with my family."

And so it is, sometimes the things that matter the least are costing us the things that matter the most. Don't let this happen to you.

Now pause and breathe in ... Breathe out, with a HINT of a smile. WOW. Looks GOOD on you. Y-E-A-H.

FUNOMENAL™ Positivity Best Practice: I invite you TODAY to pause and answer these value clarification questions for yourself. Write the questions down, followed by your answers.

Be sure to complete the three sentences at the end: I'm beginning to suspect ___. It's becoming clear that ___. Something I CAN and WILL do is ___. And then do it. Do it TODAY.

Had I not done this exercise, I would have been in danger of missing out on the beauty of my wife and the youth of my children by getting distracted by other things that really didn't matter as much.

"Regularly review what's most important to you. Don't let a BIG bag of nothing cost you a BIGGER bag of SOMETHING." - Tony Brigmon

Build a Dream Team the Southwest Airlines Way

Years ago at Southwest Airlines, I had the pleasure of doing 17 presentations with Dr. Jody Hoffer Gittell, author of *The Southwest Airlines Way* book.

Based on Jody's research, she discovered three things Southwest Airlines had that the other airlines didn't that attributed to our success. Shared goals, shared knowledge, and mutual respect.

Yes. We had shared goals. If the dream is not a team dream, you cannot have a dream team. But what you WILL have is a nightmare. Only this one will be real. We had shared goals.

We shared our knowledge. We have two responsibilities in life: 1. Learn something new. 2. Share it with those who have an interest. We did this at Southwest Airlines because we truly believed "none of us was as smart as all of us."

This helped us keep reinventing ourselves while the other airlines were trying to catch up with us.

And we had mutual respect. Everyone had an important part to play. And if each of us didn't play our part well, it reflected on all of us. Intuitively we knew you get a better return with the boomerang of respect than with the hand grenade of disrespect.

It wasn't an US vs THEM environment. No, it was WE. We taught our new hires "When I becomes We, our success is guaranteed." And it was. Our competition didn't stand a chance.

And so it is that with shared goals, shared knowledge, and mutual respect you can accomplish incredible things in both your personal and professional relationships.

Shared goals make you strong. Shared knowledge makes you smarter. Mutual respect brings you closer. It's the triple threat, with no regrets.

Now pause and breathe in ... Breathe out, with a HINT of a smile. WOW. Looks GOOD on you. Y-E-A-H.

FUNOMENAL™ Positivity Best Practice: I invite you TODAY to sit down with your team, whether it be with your significant other or with your team at the office and discuss how you're doing with shared goals, shared knowledge, and mutual respect.

If you're not doing as well as you'd like, fix it with the help of the team. Together you can do this. Apart you cannot.

"If the dream is not a team dream, you cannot have a Dream Team. But what you will have is a nightmare. Only this one will be real." - Tony Brigmon

Boost Happiness with Smile Stories

One day, at Kroger Grocery Store's self-checkout, I decided to have a little spontaneous fun. When I got home, I felt impressed to share my experience on Facebook.

I wrote, "Just had a delightful chat with the automated female voice at the self-checkout at Kroger. She thanked me for being a valued customer. I thanked her for thanking me and complimented her for having such a cheerful voice.

"I could tell it caught her off guard because she didn't know what to say. But I suspect she really liked it."

The response to my sharing this Smile story was super. Lots of 'likes.' One attorney friend replied he burst out laughing when he read my post.

On another occasion, I was to speak at a medical auxiliary in Austin, Texas. A lady named Lynn Harris, who didn't know me, was asked by the Meeting Planner to pick me up at the airport. She showed up with a sign that read, "Are you Tony?"

As the men came off the escalator she would step forward with her sign and smile and ask, "Are you Tony?" She reported to me that the first three guys said, "NO." But the fourth said, "I COULD be." And I was the fifth.

I share this Smile story with my audiences, adding, "So if you're single and looking for an interesting way to meet interesting people, just show up at the airport with your sign. Based on the research of Lynn Harris, one out of four people you meet will want to explore possibilities with you, and the fifth one will be the REAL DEAL." And my audiences laugh and love it.

And so it is. Smile stories make people smile and even laugh out loud. Whether you're sharing your story or listening to someone else share theirs, it brings more positivity into everyone's lives.

Now pause and breathe in ... Breathe out, with a HINT of a smile. WOW. Looks GOOD on you. Y-E-A-H.

FUNOMENAL™ Positivity Best Practice: In all likelihood, there is something that happened today or yesterday that made you smile or laugh. Share it TODAY with someone around you and it'll make them smile or laugh as well.

I asked my wife, a substitute teacher, "Did anything happen today that made you smile or laugh?"

She said, "Yes." And then she told me about a little first grader who's a loner and doesn't interact with anyone, and how he just out of the blue came up and gave her a BIG hug. It made her smile. It made me smile too.

Smile stories are contagious and can work wonders for positive attitudes. Share your smile stories and invite others to share theirs. Do it TODAY.

Be FUNOMENAL™: have more fun, get more done, and bring out the best in everyone. You can do this.

"Share what made you smile or laugh out loud. Invite others to do the same. Smile Stories boost happiness and productivity." - Tony Brigmon

How to Decide What's Important

I used to have a lot of difficulty deciding the most important thing to do on a long list of things I needed to do. A friend of mine suggested I use the "Bubble Up - Bubble Down" approach.

I said, "What in the world is that?" He replied, "Bubble Up - Bubble Down is only the fastest way to decide what's most important from any list. The brain can decide quickly between two things, but not quickly between more than two. So, decide between two things at a time.

"The winner bubbles up to the top. The loser bubbles down to the bottom.

"Let's say you have five things on your to-do list and you need to decide which is most important. Compare the first two. Which one wins? Item #2? Good, it bubbles up to the top. It's now #1. Then compare the 3rd item to #1. The new #1 still wins? Good. It stays at the top.

"Now compare #4 to #1. #4 wins? Boom! It bubbles to the top. It's now #1. And now compare #5 to #1. #1 still wins? It stays at the top. Now you know what's MOST important. How about that?

"Overall, it takes less time to decide with Bubble Up - Bubble Down because you're only deciding between two things at a time. And it moves quickly."

And so it is, studies show that on average, Americans make 70 choices a day. So it's easy to see why some people can be indecisive. Cutting down on choices is the best way to make better decisions.

Choice overload reduces engagement, decision quality, and satisfaction. We end up walking away or deciding not to choose because it's too hard to figure out what's best. That's why Bubble Up - Bubble Down works so well.

No matter how much you have on your list, you're only deciding between two things at a time. Easy breezy. Bada-bing, Bada-boom.

Now pause and breathe in ... Breathe out, with a HINT of a smile. WOW. Looks GOOD on you. Y-E-A-H.

FUNOMENAL™ Positivity Best Practice: I invite you TODAY, whether you have three things on your To-Do list, or 10, or more, use Bubble Up-Bubble Down to quickly get to what's MOST important. You'll be glad you did. It'll not only help you decide faster; you'll make better decisions too. Do it TODAY.

"Decide between only two things at a time and let the winner take on the next choice. This is the quickest path to the best choice." - Tony

Tap the Wisdom of Others for Your Gain

I was talking with a friend. I'll call him Jerry because that's his name. He's a successful entrepreneur. The thought came to me one day to ask him for his success formula.

I said, "Jerry, if I were your son just starting my career, what advice would you give me?"

He appeared intrigued by the way I asked the question and smiled and said, "Three things: Play your own game. Make your own rules. Quit when you're ahead." In other words, there's a time to hang it up before you get hung up going way past your prime.

WOW. What a GREAT success formula. I couldn't get it out of my mind. And Jerry's wisdom, based on his life experience, was mine for the asking, by simply knowing how to ask in an intriguing way, and then listen respectfully to all he had to say.

Jerry's success formula later helped inspire me to make my dream -- of becoming Southwest Airlines Ambassador of Fun -- come true.

And so it is, everyone has wisdom to share with you. Some of it will come from their successes. But often, the most valuable wisdom comes from their failures. Their wisdom can save you a lot of pain -- if you have the courage to ask and the willingness to listen.

The most powerful two seconds you can give anyone is a two-second pause after you've listened to all they have to share with you. It's those two seconds that CONVINCE them they have been heard.

And once they're convinced of that, oh my goodness, they'll share more great things with you!

Now pause and breathe in ... Breathe out, with a HINT of a smile. WOW. Looks GOOD on you. Y-E-A-H.

FUNOMENAL™ Positivity Best Practice: Do this TODAY: Play your own game. Make sure what you're doing TODAY is what you do best and delegate the rest.

Make your own rules: Test things out for yourself to see what does and doesn't work for you. And they'll be YOUR rules, not someone else's.

Quit when you're ahead: When what you do stops fulfilling you, move on to something else that does.

And most importantly, TODAY, get in the habit of asking people you respect and admire to share their wisdom or best advice with you.

A question that has served me well is, "If I were your son, what would you advise me to do?"

You'll be amazed at the wisdom you'll accumulate through the insights of so many who are willing to share with you, because you knew how to ask and how to listen. Then, you can share what you've learned with those who know how to ask and how to listen to YOU.

"Exchange best advice in five words or less with others. Everyone walks away feeling better and wiser." - Tony Brigmon

How to Inspire Others to Remain Loyal to You

One day, I got a call from the President of the Infomart in Dallas about a challenge the company was facing. The challenge was they had three employee groups that had merged from three different companies. They didn't interact well with each other.

It was a classic US vs. THEM scenario. What complicated the problem even more was that NONE of the three groups trusted management, so they wouldn't communicate what their issues really were so they could be addressed.

They arranged for me to do one of my "Are We Having FUN, Yet?" presentations. They hoped that if these three groups had some fun together, it might help them become more open to working better together and build trust toward management.

The plan worked, with ONE exception. They did have FUN together, but they still didn't trust management. However, they now trusted ME. They communicated that if the company would arrange for the managers to leave the room, they would tell ME the truth about their issues. So the company agreed.

I asked the employees what they wanted, but were not getting from management. It was a group consensus: "communication and organization." I explored what that meant to them and set up a meeting with the managers.

Acting on a hunch, I asked the managers the two things they felt were their greatest strengths as managers. Guess what they said? Yep. Communication and organization.

And so it is. There's something about having fun together that removes barriers to working better together and to being honest with someone they can trust.

Now pause and breathe in ... Breathe out, with a HINT of a smile. WOW. Looks GOOD on you. Y-E-A-H.

FUNOMENAL™ Positivity Best Practice: Starting TODAY, I invite you to think of ways you can have more fun together in your personal and professional relationships. If there are trust issues, find someone everyone can trust so the truth can be revealed and the problems addressed and solved.

Here are two great questions you can use to build trust personally and professionally: 1. Is there anything I've done in the last 30-90 days that would cause you to want to leave me? And, 2. Is there anything I've done that would cause you to want to stay?

Then stop doing the LEAVE things and start doing more of the STAY things. Do it TODAY.

"Those who have fun together can get more done together. If you want serious results, it pays to take fun seriously." - Tony Brigmon

Three Wishes That Make Happiness Come True

Someone once told me (okay, it could have been me because I talk to myself a lot) to be careful what you wish for others. Because it boomerangs back to you with interest. So it only makes sense to wish positive things for others, right? Right.

Here are three wishes I discovered that have done wonders for me in terms of boosting my daily happiness and productivity. And they've been especially helpful to me in dealing with negative situations.

These three wishes can also serve: as a powerful road-rage remedy, an energizing nonverbal wish for those you see out and about, and a delightful verbal wish in the presence of someone you care about.

As a fast-positive-powerful FUNOMENAL™ Positivity Best Practice, this one is hard to beat. Here are the three wishes:

1. May you be well.
2. May you be happy.
3. May you have more than enough of all the GOOD stuff.

You can even use these three wishes (or statements) as a daily writing meditation exercise to put your brain in a positive mental state to kick-start your day the right way.

It doesn't take long to do. But you'll notice the positive effects linger with you long after you do. That's what I've noticed.

Writing by hand focuses your attention in a way that is much more effective than simply reading, hearing, or reciting affirmations. Yes, typing them works too.

Kindness to others begins with kindness to self, so I mentally include myself as I write, "This is for each and everyone everywhere" followed by the three statements or wishes.

Several days into doing this writing exercise, not only did I notice I was feeling happier, but also my relationships with others were becoming even kinder and more positive.

Example: I found that what I was wishing for everyone else was doing great things for me, not only in terms of my personal happiness but also in terms of my productivity.

Wishing positives for others put my brain in a positive mental state, and in that state, I found I was more courageous in facing difficulties, more willing to help others, and more interested in their well-being and happiness. How about that!

Helpful insights came to me daily as I wrote these three wishes. I'll share a few with you here.

"May you be well." When I'm not feeling well, I don't have the emotional strength to fight off negative emotions, and it's easier for them to take me over. That's when I say and do things I later regret. Ouch.

"May you be happy." When I'm not happy about something, it's difficult to see the good in anything. Not good. That's when depressing thoughts show up to take me down. Then other negative thoughts and emotions are attracted to the kill (the kill of my positive emotions).

"May you have more than enough of all the GOOD stuff." When I don't have enough of something I really need, it can be depressing. And I'm not just talking about money here. When I have more than enough, I can share with others, which is a great antidote for depression.

I want people to have these three wishes because of what it will do for them and because of what it will do for the rest of us who have to interact with them.

I want them to be "well" so they can feel more positive about themselves and what they can accomplish.

I want them to be "happy" because going around acting like they were weaned on a pickle doesn't make them or anyone who sees them any happier.

I want them to have "more than enough of all the GOOD stuff" so they can feel like the richest of souls when they share the extra with others who need it.

These three wishes for others have turned out to be a great road-rage remedy for me as well. Immediately wishing them for other drivers, when they do fascinating things in traffic, helps me keep negative emotions about their driving from taking me over.

And wishing the other drivers well will add more to my positive mental state than honking and giving them non-verbal gestures. Really. I've done the math.

You'll be amazed at how this positive road-rage remedy best practice calms negative emotions and puts a smile back on your face to share with loved ones when you arrive home.

Wishing others well -- silently or verbally -- charges my "positivity" battery so I am more productive and can deal better with negatives that show up in my life.

I not only do this with people I see in person, but even with those I see on the news on TV. I'm always amazed at how doing this changes my attitude for better toward them.

Now pause and breathe in ... Breathe out, with a HINT of a smile. WOW. Looks GOOD on you. Y-E-A-H.

FUNOMENAL™ Positivity Best Practice: TODAY, I invite you to do this energizing best practice both as a writing exercise to kick-start your day and as a mental-verbal energizer as you go about your day.

As a writing exercise, you can simply copy these three wishes by hand in a notebook or journal, or on your electronic device.

Make it a daily routine. You're gonna love what this does for you and your relationships, especially your interactions with difficult people.

It can also help heal wounds from your past as you become calmer and more understanding, forgiving, and compassionate.

Please don't accept or reject my excitement about this fun best practice until you've tried it. You'll be amazed at how wishing others well boosts your happiness and productivity, and enhances your relationships. Do it TODAY.

"What you wish for others tends to boomerang back to you, with interest. May your wildest dreams come true. Woo hoo." - Tony Brigmon

Use the Three Views Technique to Achieve Anything

One day, I was listening to my son's karate instructor explain the importance of understanding and applying the Three VIEWS to become a better martial artist. He referred to them as the Preview, the View, and the Review.

In the Preview, he said, you see yourself having won the match and how that would feel. You also see yourself doing the specific things that would win the match.

The View he described as right NOW and the goal in the View is to focus your full attention on what's happening in front of you right NOW, so you can deal effectively with it.

He described the Review as the part where you review exactly what happened so you can learn and grow from it, no matter what happened.

I was hooked. I began to apply the Preview, the View, and the Review in all aspects of my life. My Preview of being Southwest Airlines Ambassador of FUN led to impressions that I could immediately act on in the View. The Review taught me what to start, stop, or continue doing.

And I did these things until my Preview became my Review. And my Preview became true: I was Southwest Airlines Official Ambassador of FUN.

I was also able to use the Preview, the View, and the Review to lose over 70 pounds of me that my wife wasn't legally married to, as I shared with you earlier. It helped me get past procrastination, and to do things that I was glad to have done.

When uninvited emotions like depression, anger, and fear showed up, I could use the Preview, the View, and the Review to get through those bad boys too.

And so it is, what you see yourself doing over time, you will find yourself doing at the right time. The Preview, the View, and the Review can create a better View for you. Believe it.

Now pause and breathe in ... Breathe out, with a HINT of a smile. WOW. Looks GOOD on you. Y-E-A-H.

FUNOMENAL™ Positivity Best Practice: We'll explore one day at a time in the next three stories how to use the Preview, the View, and the Review to achieve whatever's important to you.

So for now, there's only ONE thing for you to do: decide what you want more than anything else to put in your Preview. If you do this TODAY, you'll be ready when the Preview begins to work its magic for you, like it did for me.

Be FUNOMENAL™: have more fun, get more done, and bring out the best in everyone. You can do this.

"Preview what you want. View how it is. Review how it went. Doing these Views is time well spent." - Tony Brigmon

Use the Preview to Make a Dream Come True

When I was working as a supervisor in reservations for Southwest Airlines, I'd have some interactive fun with our employees on breaks. We'd laugh together and get re-energized.

I'd pretend I was Southwest Airlines Goodwill Ambassador.

I'd say something like, "Ladies and gentlemen, here he is. You all know him. We all love him. Can't get enough of him, please help me welcome Southwest Airlines Goodwill Ambassador, Tony Brigmon.
H-e-r-e's Tony!" They'd laugh and clap and I'd share some interactive fun with them.

It wasn't long into these imaginary introductions before I began to get impressions of actual things I could do to make my dream a reality. The first impression was to call a friend, Mike Murray, who had a unique ability to write attention-getting proposals.

Mike helped me create a question-and-answer proposal that anticipated some of the questions that the then-President Howard Putnam might ask me; therefore, I would intrigue him long enough to hear me out as to what I proposed to do, and how it would benefit Southwest Airlines.

So, I checked that action item off my To-Do list. I had a proposal.

The next impression I received was to spontaneously call Mr. Putnam's office. He didn't know me and I had never met him. I wasn't sure what to say when his secretary Sherry Phelps answered the phone.

But what I heard myself say was, "Sherry, would you please tell Mr. Putnam I'm on the line. Tell him I've got the answer, but I'm not quite sure about the question."

She laughed and said, "Are you serious?" I laughed and said, "I think I am." She put me on hold and told Mr. Putnam what I said. He laughed and said, "I'd like to hear the answer. Have him come over to my office TODAY after he gets off his shift."

That meeting led to a six-month trial as Southwest Airlines Goodwill Ambassador and to my becoming their official Ambassador of FUN.

And so it is. A dream-come-true begins with an energizing Preview, which leads to an impression of what you can do.

If you act immediately on the first impression, it leads to another, and finally to the achievement of your DREAM, which will give you more satisfaction than you can possibly imagine!

Now pause and breathe in ... Breathe out, with a HINT of a smile. WOW. Looks GOOD on you. Y-E-A-H.

FUNOMENAL™ Positivity Best Practice: TODAY I invite you to Preview what you'd love to find yourself having and doing. Preview the end. Try it on to see if it fits or feels right. That's where the momentum begins.

Next, see yourself doing what it would take to make it happen. If you do this and act immediately on the impressions that follow, you'll find your Preview becomes your View. Do it TODAY.

"Preview having what you want and doing what it would take to get it. Act immediately on the impressions that come. Got it? Get it." - Tony Brigmon

Use the View to Handle Whatever's in Front of You

One day, I walked into the kitchen and saw the sink and counter filled with dirty dishes. My wife had a chart on the wall indicating whose turn it was to WASH the dishes. Guess what? It was MY turn.

She expected all six of our children and me to take turns. Someone before me had NOT taken their turn. The words of the line, "I brought you into this world and I can take you out!" came to mind.

But instead, I said to myself, "Well, there's only ONE thing TO do: Walk to the sink." So I mindfully did that. Then I said, "NOW there's only ONE thing to do: Fill it with water." I did that.

And then I said, "Now there's only ONE thing to do: Put in the detergent." And the next thing you know with my "only ONE thing to do" approach it was all done. And I was amazed at how good I was still feeling, compared to other dish-washing adventures.

This experience later inspired a fun song I wrote called, "Focus On One, Have More Fun. Look at it All and You Climb the Wall."

And so it is, the View is this very moment right now. It's what's in front of you. And in the View, right NOW, there's never more than ONE thing to do, because that's all you CAN do right now.

And when you begin the next ONE thing, the Miracle of Momentum kicks in and takes you all the way through the task to the end.

So when you do your Preview and you get an impression for the View, there's only ONE thing to do: Act on it immediately: Begin. It is what it is till it ain't. You can make it better.

If there's a positive in the View, say thank you. If there's a negative in the View, there's only ONE thing to do: Face it courageously and begin the next ONE thing.

Now pause and breathe in ... Breathe out, with a HINT of a smile. WOW. Looks GOOD on you. Y-E-A-H.

FUNOMENAL™ Positivity Best Practice: TODAY, I invite you to focus on ONE thing and have more fun. ONE thing at a time, no matter how much you have on your plate. Take ONE of those things, just ONE, and give it your full attention.

NO, don't glance over at the rest of it, or you'll climb the wall. How do you eat an elephant? That's right, ONE bite at a time.

When faced with a daunting task or project, first ask yourself, "How would it feel if this were already done?" If the honest answer is, "It would feel GOOD," then that means it would be a GOOD thing to do.

So now, there's only ONE thing to do: The next ONE thing. Do it NOW. Do it TODAY.

"There's only ONE thing to do: the next ONE thing in front of you. Begin. Momentum kicks in and takes you the end. DONE. FUN." - Tony Brigmon

How to do the Review for a New or Improved View

On September 21, 1982, I received an eight-page evaluation from a professional speaker's evaluator who had been highly recommended by someone I respected. I asked for and arranged to pay him for his help because I wanted to get better as a keynote speaker.

This was my first evaluation after he watched me do a presentation.

He wrote: "Tony, you had a tough audience here, and I think you handled them well. What impressed me most was your potential as a speaker. I knew you were good. I wasn't aware of how good you CAN be.

"You can be great, Tony. Your willingness to work, coupled with your talent, can take you as far as you want to go in the speaking industry. Although much of what you did was appropriate for this audience, my evaluation still contains some negative comments.

"It just seems to me you are destined for bigger things with audiences of upper-level employees, who are already doing well but want to improve. So, If I seem overly critical, it's only because I'm anticipating larger, more stimulating, and more discriminating audiences.

"My evaluation is divided into three parts: Strengths, Weaknesses, and Suggestions."

This was the first of many evaluations I have received throughout my career. Acting on ALL of his suggestions accelerated my improvement as a professional speaker.

In fact, I was later blessed to be one of only 10 speakers featured by Meetings and Conventions Magazine in an article entitled: "Most Wanted -- Hottest Speakers on the Circuit Right Now!"

And so it is. Feedback is the "breakfast of champions." Ask for it. This will make people feel safer about sharing the truth with you. And the truth can set you free to be all you can be. There are some things you can't see that others CAN. Let them help you get better. You'll have their support and applause when you do.

Now pause and breathe in ... Breathe out, with a HINT of a smile. WOW. Looks GOOD on you. Y-E-A-H.

FUNOMENAL™ Positivity Best Practice: TODAY, I invite you to make the Review part of everything you do, no matter how well you do it now. Pick something TODAY you want to improve. Find someone whose opinions you respect, and who has an eye for observation and evaluation.

Ask them to help you. Their feedback probably won't cost you a penny. Just a heartfelt thank you will do. And if you do that part well, you'll earn the right to their willingness to help you improve.

Three review questions I recommend are: What went well? What would make it better? Anything else that might be good for me to do?

Remember to thank them every time, whether you agree with them or not. Just say, "Thank you." This will increase the chances of their helping you again. Do it TODAY.

"Do a Review after everything you do. It leads to better plans and to greater views." - Tony Brigmon

How to Stop Fear from Robbing You of What You Were Made to Do

In November of 2014, I received an email from Sara, Vice President and Director of Content Strategies with Avanoo.

Avanoo partners with more than 200 of the world's most renowned experts, authors, and speakers to create their course content, which consists of visual images, music, and story messages.

The result: 94% employee approval rate of their videos, and performance improvement more than 10 times what clients have seen in other video programs.

Sara wrote: "I saw your website and your work seems perfectly aligned with programs on OUR website that our community has been ASKING for."

I was intrigued. A conference call was arranged with Daniel, Co-Founder of Avanoo. We had a delightful conversation. He asked me GREAT questions. That call led to a final chat with Avanoo's other co-founder Prosper.

A Noo is a 3-minute (or less) story, enhanced by the Avanoo researched-based format of visual images and music.

On the call with Prosper, the more he talked about the required detailed structure needed for a Noo, the more discouraged I became -- because I have A.D.D. That's right. I'm an "Attention Deficit Dis-Oh, is that a butterfly?" kind of guy. And fear was telling me, "You can't be creative with all this structure, and besides, you don't have enough content for 30 Noos."

Prosper, hearing the discouragement in my voice, asked me just before we hung up, "How will you KNOW you can't do this if you don't give it a try?"

As I thought about it overnight, FEAR raised its ugly head and said what fear says. So, the next morning I sent an email to Daniel, copying Prosper and Sara, turning DOWN the invitation to be a contributing author.

Daniel replied simply saying, "About your not having enough stories: People have thought that before and it's NEVER the case. YOU are a creative machine. You'll find the content."

And Prosper's "How will you KNOW if you don't give it a try?" question would NOT leave me alone. So, I decided to give it a go.

After submitting several stories, I received a note from Prosper, saying: "You were MADE for creating Noos!" This gave me hope.

So here we are, LOTS of stories later. Daniel was right. I found the content. Prosper was right. I AM made for creating Noos. And how about FUNOMENAL you? What are YOU made for? I know you were made for something special. Everyone is.

Now pause and breathe in ... Breathe out, with a HINT of a smile. WOW. Looks GOOD on you. Y-E-A-H.

FUNOMENAL™ Positivity Best Practice: I invite you TODAY to do what you were made to do. If you don't know what it is yet, don't let fear rob you from finding it and enjoying a delightful destiny. You'll know it when you feel it.

In fact, fear may be introducing you to it NOW. But you won't know for sure unless you face it and give it try. Be FUNOMENAL™: have more fun, get more done, and bring out the best in everyone. You can do this.

"Don't let FEAR rob you of what you were made to do. Begin and watch fear step aside for you." - Tony Brigmon

Smile & Wave

Make someone's day!

Use Communication 101 to Resolve Conflict

One day at work, my boss criticized me in the presence of some other employees. It embarrassed me. And A.D.D. guys like me tend to make things much more than they really are.

So, to keep myself from going off on my boss and getting fired, I stepped out into the hall to calm down. About that time, the president of the company (who knew and liked me) walked by. He quickly observed that I was not my normal cheerful self.

He said, "What's wrong?" To which I replied, "My problem is how to tell you what's wrong without getting myself or anyone else in trouble." He assured me that wouldn't happen.

So, I told him about being embarrassed by my boss in front of others. The president said, "Let's fix this. Here's what I want you to do. The next time he does that, follow him back into his office. Close and lock the door.

"Walk over to him, holding up your fist and say, 'I have some feedback for you. And if you interrupt me, I'm going to rearrange your face.' Then tell him what he did and how you'd like for him to handle it next time."

I said, "If I say and do that, he'll fire me." He said, "Really? Who's HIS boss?" I said, "Well, YOU are." He said, "That's right. He won't fire you. DO it."

Sure enough, he did it again that same afternoon. So I followed the president's advice step by step. When I got to, "If you interrupt me, I'm going to rearrange your face" my boss immediately sat down with a startled look on his face and said, "I won't interrupt you."

I communicated what he did that bothered me and how I'd like for him to handle it next time. To my shock, he stood up, shook my hand and said, "It'll never happen again." And it didn't. He and I became friends and remained that way thanks to Communication 101.

And so it is. Knowing what to say, when to say it, how to say it, and how to listen while it is being said is something you can learn to do very well. And it begins with paying attention very well when others say things, and then making a note of it.

Now pause and breathe in ... Breathe out, with a HINT of a smile. WOW. Looks GOOD on you. Y-E-A-H.

FUNOMENAL™ Positivity Best Practice: TODAY, I invite you to begin practicing the right words to use in resolving conflict. Hint: It probably won't be, "If you interrupt me I'm going to rearrange your face!", but if that is what it takes, so be it. You have to go with what feels right and works.

When you hear someone communicate something very well verbally or in writing, make a note of it. Then you can review it, practice it, and make it yours. And later you can access it to resolve difficult situations.

You can even Google Communication 101 and begin practicing the sound bites that are a good fit for you. The more you practice the words, the more comfortable they'll be to use in uncomfortable communication situations.

And for that time when all else fails, and unacceptable behavior is occurring, try this proven one, "What you're saying or doing is unacceptable to me. I'm open to working this out with you when you're able to do so reasonably. I'm now leaving to protect myself. I'm sorry."

Start practicing Communication 101 TODAY.

"You get more mileage out of, 'I've got a problem and I need your help.' than ignoring the problem and getting no help." - Tony Brigmon

Use the Carrot and the Stick for Best Results

Three days after I made my initial proposal to Howard Putnam, CEO of Southwest Airlines, to become their Goodwill Ambassador, he called me in to discuss his decision.

He said, "Here are the terms. We're going to give you six months to generate in a measurable way the PR you claim you can. If you are successful, you will become our official Goodwill Ambassador. If you are unsuccessful you will lose your current job as supervisor and start all over with the company with day one pay, day one seniority.

Talk about a BIG carrot and a BIG stick. My dream was to become their Goodwill Ambassador, so the carrot was perfect. The stick? My employee number was 1,259 and the thought of having to start all over with Southwest Airlines with day one pay and seniority was SCARY indeed. WOW!

But the carrot prevailed. Yet the stick was there to keep me on track every day as a motivation to give this my very best shot. Turns out they were both just what I needed, because six months later the measurable feedback received from civic and service group Meeting Planners proved that what I was doing was a BIG hit with all of these organizations.

Mr. Putnam called me in and announced that the trial was over and that I was now Southwest Airlines Official Goodwill Ambassador. Woo hoo. That title later evolved into Ambassador of Fun, which gave me more joy than you can possibly imagine.

Did I ever reveal the terms of the "'trial'" to my wife? No way. Her need for job security, and the fear of possibly losing it on something as risky as this, would have immobilized me.

When it was a done deal and I revealed the "job-on-the-line" terms of the trial, she was shocked, but happy and proud of me.

And so it is, with the right carrot and the right stick anyone can be motivated to do their best. Howard Putnam intuitively knew the right ones for me and used them masterfully.

Recently I reminded him of this experience and he said, "Surely, I was kidding when I set the start-all-over terms!" I said, "If you were kidding, you sure fooled me." We both laughed.

When you combine the appropriate carrot and stick to motivate others, it works best. Not all carrots and sticks work, but the ones tailored to what they want or fear most usually do.

Now pause and breathe in ... Breathe out, with a HINT of a smile. WOW. Looks GOOD on you. Y-E-A-H.

FUNOMENAL™ Positivity Best Practice: TODAY, I invite you to find out what someone's carrot and stick is and use them to help them give the best effort. And remember it has to be THEIR carrot and THEIR stick, not yours, for this to work best.

These two questions can help: What will you get if you do this? (Carrot) What will it cost you if you don't? (Stick) A good WHY answers both questions. Sometimes just asking these questions is all it takes to get motivated. Do it TODAY.

"Review the GAIN if you do it and the PAIN if you don't and you'll do it. The carrot AND the stick: your double whammy. Do it." - Tony Brigmon

Look at Your Work Through the Eyes of the Owner

Before coming to work for Southwest Airlines, Dallas YMCA leader Jack Semones offered me some temporary work on a property he was managing. He gave me an assignment of things he'd like done and then left me to it.

I had finished early, and I was sitting on a brick wall with my feet dangling over the side when he returned close to lunchtime. Jack called out to me and said, "Come get in the truck and we'll go have some lunch."

Before we pulled away he gestured at the property and said, "If you were the owner of this property and were going to hire someone to do some work for you, what would you have them do, based on what you see right now?"

I began to point out things I'd have someone do. I said, "I'd have them pull those dead limbs out of the pond and clear those weeds away over there" and so forth.

Jack then said, "When I pulled up I saw you had finished early and that's commendable. You're a good worker. But the one who's going to get ahead in life is the one who looks at the work through the eyes of the owner and then does the things the owner would do without having to be told by the owner to do them."

He said, "If you had someone working for you, would you want them working at a furious pace or a steady pace?" I said, "Steady pace." Jack said, "That's right because 'steady' finishes and wins the race."

Jack then pulled a handkerchief out of his pocket and said, "Back in the day when I finished early, I'd pull out this handkerchief and begin cleaning the headlights and taillights on the truck, working at a calm, steady pace.

"Looking at my work through the eyes of the owner has served me well over the years."

And so it is. When you look at your job through the eyes of the owner and do the things that need to be done, you earn a reputation that will take you as far as you want to go with any organization.

This principle served me well when I went to work at Southwest Airlines, where I earned a good reputation for my work ethic.

Now pause and breathe in ... Breathe out, with a HINT of a smile. WOW. Looks GOOD on you. Y-E-A-H.

FUNOMENAL™ Positivity Best Practice: TODAY, I invite you to look at what you do through the eyes of the owner and do what needs to be done without having to be told to do it. If you ARE the owner, teach someone what Jack Semones taught me so they too can benefit from his advice.

"Look at your work through the eyes of the owner. Do what they would do. They'll like what they view and see a keeper in you." - Tony Brigmon

Use YOUR Stories to Communicate Powerfully

At the beginning of my speaking career, I had the delightful experience of spending a day with a man whose unique ability was to help speakers discover and tell their own stories well for maximum impact with their audiences. His name was Bill.

I was 30 years old at the time. Bill opened our meeting with, "Let's find your stories because that's where the power of communication is. Let's talk about your good, bad, and ugly experiences from birth to age 10." So I started talking and he started taking notes on 3-by-5 cards.

At the end of those stories, he said, "Now let's go from age 10 to age 20, good, bad, and ugly." I talked. He kept taking FAST notes.

And finally, he said, "Okay, let's go from age 20 to age 30." I told my stories while he scribbled away.

At the end of this exercise, he picked up the phone and called someone he knew in an office close by. He said, "Got any employees over there right now?" The guy said, "Yep." Bill said, "Good, I'm bringing over Southwest Airlines new Goodwill Ambassador (This title later evolved into Ambassador of FUN) with his brand new presentation. No charge."

When he hung up, I said, "I don't have a brand new presentation." He said, "Sure you do. I've been taking notes. You've got some great stories." We then reviewed each story including the moral of the story, and so forth. He handed me the cards and said, "Let's go."

I told my stories to the group. They loved them. Bill called another group from that office and arranged for me to tell my stories again. While going from the first group to the second, he evaluated my storytelling. He suggested I get into dialogue and action as quickly as possible to keep the stories moving.

By the end of the day, I had told my stories to three different groups and they kept getting better and better. These stories assured my success as Southwest Airlines Ambassador of FUN.

And so it is. You've had good, bad, and ugly experiences. Each of them is a story with a moral to it. Each one also has a Best Practice to share with others on either what to do or what not to do next time. You can use them to communicate powerfully with others. No one can tell YOUR Stories as powerfully as you can.

And remember a picture may be worth a thousand words. But a great story can be worth a thousand pictures.

Now pause and breathe in ... Breathe out, with a HINT of a smile. WOW. Looks GOOD on you. Y-E-A-H.

FUNOMENAL™ Positivity Best Practice: TODAY, I invite you to think of a recent good, bad, ugly or funny experience. Write it out. How did it begin? What happened next? How did it end? What's the moral of the story? What's the Best Practice to repeat or avoid next time?

Use YOUR stories to communicate powerful messages TODAY.

"A picture may be worth a thousand words, but a good story is worth a thousand pictures. Use stories to teach and inspire." - Tony Brigmon

Use the First 15 Seconds for Rapport and More

I once heard someone I respect say, "Whatever you want someone or a group to do, have them do it within the first 15 seconds of your initial interaction with them and they'll cooperate with you."

I found that idea fascinating and decided to put it to the test with an audience I was about to address.

I wanted them to feel safe doing what I asked them to do, interact with one another, and have fun together. So I thought, "What could I get them to do within the first 15 seconds that would accomplish all three of these things?"

When you ask yourself these kinds of questions, guess what? You get answers.

This is what came to me to do. As soon as I was introduced, I walked to the microphone and said, "Would you please turn to the person next to you, shake their hand, and say, 'I feel REASONABLY good about being here.' "

To my delight they immediately felt safe doing what I asked them to do, interacted with one another, and had some fun together. The room was immediately filled with positive energy as they shook hands, said those fun words, and laughed out loud.

And from that point to the end of my presentation, my rapport with the audience became stronger and stronger, resulting in a standing ovation.

And I immediately thought, "Good Note to Self": Do this within the first 15 seconds with every audience." And this rapport technique has served me well over the years, especially with tough audiences. Like the Appeals Division of the IRS.

Turns out this 15-second energizer gave this no-nonsense group the permission they needed to let go and have some well-deserved fun together.

And so it is. The first 15 seconds is the brief window you have to set the tone of how you want someone or a group to interact with you. And if you'll give them a fun hint within that window, they'll work with you, not against you.

If you don't use this 15-second opportunity, you may lose the rapport you want or have to earn it the hard way.

Because once they get locked in, with arms crossed and with negative, neutral or stressed expressions on their faces, you've got your work cut out for you.

Now pause and breathe in ... Breathe out, with a HINT of a smile. WOW. Looks GOOD on you. Y-E-A-H.

FUNOMENAL™ Positivity Best Practice: TODAY, I invite you to make the first 15 seconds work FOR you and not against you.

Decide how you want someone or a group to interact with you and invite them to do it within the first 15 seconds of your initial interaction with them. Do it TODAY. You'll be glad you did.

Be FUNOMENAL™: have more fun, get more done, and bring out the best in everyone. You can do this.

"You have less than 60 seconds for a 1st impression, which can take years to change. Best foot forward. Make it all about them." - Tony Brigmon

Let the Kid in You Energize You and Others

Jack Benny was once quoted as saying, "Never follow a children's act." He was right. No one is funnier than kids. Art Linkletter proved this years ago with his classic show, "Kids Say the Darndest Things."

And it's true, they do. My wife and I discovered this first hand with our six children.

At Southwest Airlines, to help enliven our customer care and employee development sessions, I invited our employees to pass along any G-rated, family-friendly humor for me to share in these sessions, especially if it involved children.

Here are some examples of things they shared with me. Some of our favorites were these quotes that appeared on science exams for sixth graders. These delightful children wrote:

"H_2O is hot water and CO_2 is cold water."

"When you breathe you inspire. When you do not breathe you expire."

"Water is composed of two gins, oxygen, and hydrogen. Oxygen is pure gin. Hydrogen is gin and water."

"The body consists of three parts, the brainium, the borax and the abominable cavity. The brainium contains the brain, the borax contains the heart and lungs, and the abominable cavity contains the bowels, of which there are five: A, E, I, O, and U."

And kids can give profound advice.

Patrick, age 10: "Never trust a dog to watch your food."

Heather, age 9: "When your dad is mad at your mom and asks you, "Do I look stupid?" don't answer him."

Taylia, age 11: "When your mom is mad at your dad, don't let her brush your hair. Kyo, age 9: Never hold a dustbuster and a cat at the same time."

And finally, some thoughts from Kids On Marriage:

What do people do on a date? Lynette, age 8: "Dates are for having fun, and people should use them to get to know one another. Even boys have something to say if you listen long enough."

How do you decide who to marry? Kirsten, age 10: "No one decides before they grow up who they're gonna marry. God decides it all way before, and you get to find out later who you're stuck with."

When is it okay to kiss someone? Pam, age 7: "When they're rich!"

And so it is. No one does humor better than children. You can use it to connect with the child in everyone and boost energy, creativity, and happiness.

Now pause and breathe in ... Breathe out, with a HINT of a smile. WOW. Looks GOOD on you. Y-E-A-H.

FUNOMENAL™ Positivity Best Practice: TODAY, I invite you to download some G-rated humor from kids from the internet. Print and distribute copies to your staff or family before your next meeting. Invite each person to read one item aloud. By the time you get around the table, notice the boost in positive energy and creativity.

"Let the inner-child in you out to play and the adult in you will have a better day. Really. Let the fun begin. Everyone wins." - Tony Brigmon

Smile & Wave

Make someone's day!

The Power of a Little That Does a Lot

My senior year in high school I took Trigonometry from Mrs. Carletti. It became quickly apparent to me and to her that I was in over my head. My Louisiana fingers-and-toes math wasn't gonna get me through this class.

So Mrs. Carletti told me one day, "Look, if you'll keep trying your best and don't give me a hard time, I'll pass you, but I'm going to call in a couple of favors." I quickly agreed, "Whatever you want, I'll do it."

One Friday she asked me, "Are you going to the dance tonight?" I said, "Yes." She said, "Save me a dance." So when I arrived, I immediately asked her if she'd like to dance.

During the dance, she said, "You see those two girls over there in the corner?" I said, "Yes." She said, "I'm calling in my two favors right now. I've been chaperoning these dances since you all were sophomores and neither of those girls has ever been asked to dance. You're going to fix that right now."

"Walk over and ask each one of them to dance. They're going to be nervous. You're a funny guy. Get them laughing and dance with them. Then walk them over to their chairs after you dance, look them in the eye and say, 'Thank you for dancing with me.' "

And I did exactly what Mrs. Carletti asked, step by step. They were nervous. One of them was shaking while we danced. But I was able to get her laughing and she calmed down.

After I walked the second girl back to her seat, I glanced over at Mrs. Carletti and she was beaming at me, like Mr. Miyagi from "The Karate Kid" movie after his student had won the tournament.

As I think back over all the memories I have of high school: as an athlete, as a member of a Rock and Roll Band, as having a lead role in a musical, and other accomplishments -- the memory that warms my heart the most is the one of dancing with those two girls.

And so it is. It doesn't take a lot to do a little. But a little can mean a lot to so many, and most of all to you. Everyone is special. Treat them that way. I will be forever grateful to Mrs. Carletti for teaching me this great life lesson. And yes, I did pass Trigonometry with a C-. But I earned an A+ in Happiness. Thank you, Mrs. Carletti.

Now pause and breathe in ... Breathe out, with a HINT of a smile. WOW. Looks GOOD on you. Y-E-A-H.

FUNOMENAL™ Positivity Best Practice: TODAY, I invite you to look around for an opportunity to do some little something for someone. Something that would mean a LOT to them. What you'll discover is: it'll do even more for you. Do it. Do it TODAY.

"Treat everyone as special BECAUSE they are. It's the best way to create special memories for them and for you." - Tony Brigmon

How to Attract Good Things

My senior year in high school I was co-captain of the basketball team. Just before our district games began, my basketball coach, Amos Turner, asked me one day in practice, "What do you eat on game days?" He knew my brothers and I were being raised by a single mom who worked a full-time job and two part-time jobs to support us.

I said, "Six pieces of toast, with jelly." When Coach Turner, who was only about 5 feet 7 inches tall (but had a military background), spoke you listened. He said, "On the next game day you are to report to my home after school and eat with my wife and me. And I promise no one will ever know."

After that, I showed up on each game day and they fed me like a king: steak and potatoes, with all the trimmings. At our first district game, after the co-captains had met and shook hands at mid-court and I returned to the huddle, Coach Turner said, "Sit down. You're not going to start tonight. But I'll put you in after one minute."

I was shocked, but you didn't question Coach Turner. So I sat down for 60 seconds and then was sent into the game. The same thing happened at the next district game. And I asked Coach Turner, "What did I do wrong?" He said, "Nothing. We'll talk about it at practice tomorrow."

The next day he pulled me over to the side of the court where no one could hear us and he said, "Look, what I've been doing for you on game day, I'd do for anyone. I wanted you to remember that everyone is special and that I'm not favoring you. That's why I haven't let you start for two games.

"Understand?" And I did.

Years later, two weeks before he passed away, I had a chance to visit him and asked him if he'd ever shared with anyone that he had fed me on all those game days. He gave me that stern look of his and said, "I said I wouldn't and I didn't."

I told him I remembered Mrs. Turner never had steak with us on those game days, and I learned that the steak I was eating was hers. Tears came to my eyes.

At Coach Turner's funeral, many came forth to share private acts of kindness that he had done for them as well, like paying for prom suits, and so forth.

And so it is. When you do an act of kindness privately, you know happiness and will be remembered fondly long after you're gone.

Now pause and breathe in ... Breathe out, with a HINT of a smile. WOW. Looks GOOD on you. Y-E-A-H.

FUNOMENAL™ Positivity Best Practice: TODAY, I invite you to look for a way to help someone on the condition they keep it between you and them. And notice what happens after you do, not just to them, but to you. Do it TODAY.

"Private acts of kindness find ways to openly and generously pay you back. With interest. Paying it forward pays best." - Tony Brigmon

Be Prepared, Not Paranoid

A friend of mine at Southwest Airlines told me about a buddy of his who had served in Vietnam as a Green Beret. He was short and dripping wet weighed maybe around 140 pounds, but he was tough as nails.

One night he had taken his fiancée to a formal military function and on the way home they stopped at a restaurant for a bite to eat. Three local tough guys, seeing this little guy dressed in a Green Beret uniform, decided to walk over and have some fun at his expense.

One of them said to him, "You know what we're gonna do? We're gonna take you outside and whip you, Mr. Green Beret." The Green Beret smiled and said, "No you're not, because I'm gonna run. But don't you catch me. Cause I'm not gonna lose a foot race and a fight too!"

There was something about what he said, and the humorous way he said it, that sent a clear message to the bullies that this little man was prepared, and definitely not afraid of them.

So what did they do? They laughed nervously and walked away. And they lived to mess with someone else on another day. But not on this day. And not with this Green Beret.

And so it is. When you're prepared, there's nothing to fear but fear itself. So be prepared, not paranoid. When you pay the price of preparation, you earn the right to that confident sensation that you can handle whatever is in front of you.

Now pause and breathe in ... Breathe out, with a HINT of a smile. WOW. Looks GOOD on you. Y-E-A-H.

FUNOMENAL™ Positivity Best Practice: TODAY, I invite you to think of something you need to prepare for. Something that if you don't prepare well is not going to turn out well for you. What materials do you need to have? Get them.

What do you need to do to get ready? Do it. Begin. Start your preparations. The toughest part of preparation is the first step. After you take that step, it's all downhill from there. Why? Because that's when momentum kicks in and carries you to the end.

When you get to the point in your preparation where you begin to feel more excitement than fear, you are well on your way to being prepared, not paranoid. Keep going until you're more than ready.

And then you'll find success more than ready to greet you.

"Be prepared, not paranoid. The more prepared you are, the more excitement grows until it's stronger than fear." - Tony Brigmon

How to Win at Any Game

In 2015 I had the delight of participating in the BYU Scholarship Golf tournament at the Coyote Ridge Golf Course in Carrollton, Texas.

Our team had to be the oldest in the tournament with three of our four members over 60 years of age.

How did our team do? Brace yourself. We won! I'm not kidding.

Okay, two of our four are good golfers. The third player only played once a year. And I don't play at all.

So how did we win? It was a scramble tournament. For those of you, like me, who may not know what scramble means (I had to Google it) here it is.

A scramble involves four golfers playing as a team. Each player tees off and the team selects the best shot. Players then take their next shots from there. This continues until a ball is sunk. All holes are played this way.

A scramble speeds up the pace of the play and allows players of all levels to compete with each other.

Now for the amazing part. I shot 18 under par. Really. Turns out that while I'm a lousy golfer, I have an uncanny ability for finding lost golf balls. I found 36!

In my imagination, I thought of the first 18 recovered golf balls as shooting par on the course, and the next 18 as shooting 18 under. Wow. While it wasn't my official scorecard, it was my official imaginary scorecard. I was a winner! Woo hoo. Haha.

And my teammates loved it because they got extra golf balls to take home. And I had some positive memories to take home about how I contributed to their success.

And so it is. You don't have to be good at someone else's game to be a winner, or to have a good time. You just have to play your own game. Make your own rules. Quit when you're ahead! And most importantly, have fun.

Now pause and breathe in ... Breathe out, with a HINT of a smile. WOW. Looks GOOD on you. Y-E-A-H.

FUNOMENAL™ Positivity Best Practice: TODAY, I invite you to think about how you can contribute to your team at work or at home with what you do best. It may not be finding things like lost golf balls. But there is something you do well that comes easily to you.

Maybe it's your sense of humor. Or you're a good listener.

With a little bit of creativity, you can use that to serve the other members of your team. They'll love it. And they won't care if you're a lousy golfer. But they will remember how you contributed to their success.

Be FUNOMENAL™: have more fun, get more done, and bring out the best in everyone. You can do this.

"Play your own game. Make your own rules. Quit when you're ahead. You can always be a winner in your game. Play YOUR game today." - Tony

How to Fail Your Way to Success

My youngest son, Luke, was a wrestler in high school. Just before his freshman year, he decided to give wrestling a shot. He began working out with a club team during the summer.

In his first Greco-Roman/Freestyle tournament, his first opponent in the Greco part of the tournament was the defending high school folkstyle champion. It was brutal ... for my son.

His first match in the freestyle part of the tournament was against the kid who had just beaten the high school champion in the finals of Greco. It was even more brutal ... for my son.

And his third and final match of the tournament was against a kid named Speedy, who was appropriately named. He was fast and tough.

When I got down to my son on the mat, he was bleeding from his nose. He had been knocked unconscious in one of his matches. I asked him, "Are you sure you want to do this sport?"

He looked at me with a smile and said, "It can't get worse than this, right dad?" I said, "No son, I don't think so." He said, "I'd like to keep going."

And so he continued. His freshman year there was no one at his weight on the varsity, so he wrestled against experienced wrestlers. He saw the ceiling more than the mat most of that year, losing most of his matches.

But every match was filmed and reviewed with his coach. And every match he improved. His senior year his record was 55 wins with only five losses. Two of his wins were one-point victories over the Oklahoma State Champion and the Georgia State Champion.

And so it is. My son Luke is living proof you can fail your way to success, by learning from every failure. He learned more from his losses than he did from his successes. And you can do this as well.

Not only can you fail your way to success, your failures will help you appreciate and enjoy your successes.

Now pause and breathe in ... Breathe out, with a HINT of a smile. WOW. Looks GOOD on you. YEAH!

FUNOMENAL™ Positivity Best Practice: TODAY, I invite you to look back over a recent experience that went well and review what you did or didn't do that made that win possible. And record it in your success journal as a reminder of what to REPEAT.

Next, think of an experience that didn't go well and review what it was you did or didn't do that contributed to that. Record it in your success journal as a reminder of what NOT to do. And add what you plan to do instead next time. Do it TODAY.

"You can fail your way to success by learning from every failure. What did you learn?" - Tony Brigmon

How to Access the WOW in NOW!

I was having fun working at my computer creating Daily Mental Vitamins when my wife strolled into my office with a request that didn't sound like fun to me.

The request? She wanted me to dismantle the old dog house in the backyard for trash pick-up the next day. NOT my idea of fun.

I immediately noticed a surge of irritation within me, sparked by this "uninvited interruption" of my fun time. My past pattern would have been to feed this bad-boy emotion with my attention until it escalated to words I would later regret. Not fun.

Then the thought occurred to me that dismantling a dog house is a less stressful option than being IN the doghouse with my wife.

So, as I pushed my chair back to stand up, something FUNtastic within me took over. I mentally became a "reporter", broadcasting step by step what I was doing -- to an imaginary audience who couldn't see me, but could hear me.

It went like this: I am breathing in -- I am breathing out. I am smiling. I am pushing my chair back. I am standing up. I am walking out of my office -- waving a sad goodbye to my computer.

I am walking to the utility closet. I am picking up the hammer. I am walking to the dog house (Bad dog!). And so forth.

All of a sudden, right in the middle of this live "I AM" broadcast, it occurred to me that I had somehow been transported from the emotional tempest to the calm eye of the storm. I was no longer feeling upset but was actually beginning to feel happy instead.

Then came the AHA moment: "I AM" is the portal to the calm "eye" of the storm where happiness resides. WOW.

The great Chinese philosopher Lao Tzu said, "If you are depressed you are living in the past. If you are anxious you are living in the future. If you are at peace you are living in the present."

I now had the key to coming back to the peaceful present anytime I felt stress: I AM. I AM. I AM.

And you now have this I AM key as well. Repeatedly thinking or saying "I AM" brings your attention back to what you're doing -- in the NOW. The more you do this the more content, peaceful, and happy you feel.

I read a delightful article by Tara Massan. She shared a study that found a surprising predictor of happiness. She wrote:

"According to data gathered from a Harvard study group, the specific way you spend your day does not predict how happy you are. Rather, the predictive element to happiness is matching your thoughts to your action -- to have a strong mental presence of what you are doing.

"The participants in the study were surveyed via an iPhone app, which would interrupt them at random intervals and ask them what they were doing and what was on their mind.

"If a participant answered that they were not thinking about what they were doing they would answer additional questions inquiring if what they were doing was enjoyable, neutral or not enjoyable.

"The results? The data gathered by the study reveals that we tend to be at our happiest when we are thinking about what we're doing.

"For example, a person who is washing the dishes and thinking about washing the dishes is happier than a person who is washing the dishes and thinking of a future vacation."

And so it is. While thinking of something you're looking forward to (like a vacation) is a research-proven happiness booster, thinking about what you're doing makes you even happier. Go figure.

So, no matter where you go, there you are. And no matter where you are, BE THERE -- paying attention to what you're doing. You'll be happy you are. Really.

Living in the present offers you more than living in the past or future.

The two major sources of stress are:

> **Too much Past**: guilt, regret, resentment, grievances, sadness, bitterness.

> or ...

> **Too much Future**: unease, anxiety, tension, stress, worry, fear.

The WOW of NOW is:

> **The Present**: calmness, creativity, confidence, peace of mind, inspired impressions, lightness, joy, freedom, contentment, happiness, and more.

I now believe being in the present is one of the best gifts you can give yourself and others.

The dog house was dismantled. And I wasn't in it -- which gives me more satisfaction than you can possibly imagine.

Now breathe in ... breathe out with a hint of a smile. "NOW" looks good on you. WOW.

FUNOMENAL™ Positivity Best Practice: TODAY, I invite you to repeatedly use "I AM" to stay with or come back to what you are doing in the present -- but only if you want a life.

FYI: Verbally saying or mentally thinking, "I AM breathing in -- I AM breathing out" is the Mother-of-all shortcuts to the calm zone of NOW -- because the only time you can breathe is NOW.

Use "I AM" often to return to the WOW of NOW. What are YOU doing right now? Think about it.

What am I doing? I AM finishing this story. NOW.

"BOW-WOW!"

'"What am I doing?' brings your attention back to NOW, where you think better, do better, and feel better. What are you doing?" - Tony Brigmon

I Am Not IT -- Neither Are You

There's a great story told that illustrates the most important battle of our lives -- the battle between good (positive) and bad (negative) thoughts. You've likely heard or read the following story before.

An old Cherokee is teaching his grandson about life. "A fight is going on inside me," he said to the boy.

"It is a terrible fight and it is between two wolves. One is evil – he is anger, greed, fear, arrogance, and resentment."

He continued, "The other is good – he is joy, peace, love, hope, and kindness.

"The same fight is going on inside you – and inside every other person, too."

The grandson thought about it for a minute and then asked his grandfather, "Which wolf will win?"

The old Cherokee simply replied, "The one you feed."

And so it is. The way you feed positive or negative thoughts is with your attention.

Just because an uninvited negative feeling, sparked by a negative thought, shows up growling for attention doesn't mean you HAVE to feed It. You can feed the opposite part with your attention.

It is a simple concept, but not always easy to remember when the tempest is raging.

In Chinese philosophy, yin and yang (also yin-yang or yin yang "dark—bright") describe how opposite or contrary forces are actually complementary, interconnected, and interdependent in the natural world, and how they give rise to each other as they interrelate to one another.

As I read about yin and yang and the theory of opposites, this thought occurred to me: in cyclones, while the tempest is raging on the outer part, the inner part -- the "eye" -- is calm.

What if the same were true of emotions within us? What if at the same moment a negative emotion is raging there is an opposite emotion within us that is not -- just waiting to be fed with our attention to give it power over the negative one?

If part of you is upset (the tempest part), then based on the theory of opposites, there's an opposite part of you that is not (the eye of the storm part).

And if you want to get back to feeling "calm" that's the part you have to "feed" with you attention.

And if you are the "eye" (the calm part) of the storm, why not give it a name. Like "I?" Works for me.

The opposite part (the negative one) should have a name as well to avoid confusion. How about "IT?"

So, "IT" is my evil twin, huh? That guy has gotten me in a LOT of trouble. This means I am not IT. Wow. What a fascinating insight. I've always thought I was IT. Just ask my wife. Ha-ha.

Okay, so I'm not IT (And neither are YOU). But we do have to deal with IT when IT shows up -- or IT will take us over and have its stressful way with us.

Can you do this? Yes, you can. Get ready.

Now pause and breathe in ... Breathe out, with a HINT of a smile. WOW. Looks GOOD on you. Y-E-A-H.

FUNOMENAL™ **Positivity Best Practice**: TODAY, I invite you to use the "I am not IT" best practice to deal with uninvited negative emotions that surface to threaten your peace of mind and productivity. If you feed the positives, the positives will feed you. Feed the negatives, and the negatives will destroy you.

How to deal with negative emotions and feed the positive ones?

It's as simple as 1-2-3:

1. Tell the truth about IT (negative emotion). The truth sets you FREE to deal with IT. Name IT to tame IT.

2. Acknowledge the opposite (positive emotion). The positive exists within you right now -- just waiting to be fed.

3. Feed the positive with your attention until it overpowers the negative. THINK about the positive (to energize it) and watch it come to your rescue.

"Part of me (IT) is ___. (upset, angry, depressed, worried, etc) which means there's an opposite part of me that is NOT. I choose to feed the part of me that is NOT.

"I am NOT ___ (upset, angry, depressed, worried, etc). IT is. I am not IT. I am ___ (name the opposite positive emotion: calm, not angry, hopeful, confident, at peace, etc.)

You can do this. Do it TODAY.

"Just because a negative emotion is growling at you to feed it with attention, doesn't mean you have to. Feed a positive one." - Tony Brigmon

Smile
& Wave
Make someone's day!

Showdown at High Noon

Okay, it wasn't high noon, but it wasn't quite 1 pm yet, so for the sake of this story let's go with high noon.

Each month my buddy Rob and I check in on two wonderful widows to make sure they're doing okay and bring them uplifting, positive messages as part of our visit.

When we were at one of the homes yesterday, we spotted a wasp nest on one of the lady's front porch. We offered to take care of it after our visit but forgot. This morning I remembered and decided to go over there and take out years of bad wasp memories on that nest of bad boys.

My wife briefed me before my wasp-ops mission on the importance of having a good exit strategy in place. I called my friend Rob. He agreed that the exit strategy may be more important than the attack strategy.

Turns out they were both right.

This thoughtful lady had two cans of wasp spray on her porch waiting for me. She recommended I test them in the front yard before the showdown. Good advice.

Turns out the one in my left hand didn't work. Lucky for me I have a pretty good right hand, and that can was in good working order.

As our friend watched from a corner window inside her house, I moved in with the reflexes of a water buffalo, stuck in mud -- with the non-working can in my left hand (for intimidation purposes only) and the sudden death can in my right hand.

Without warning I attacked.

It was fast. It was brutal. It was deadly. A few wasps fell quietly, and several who were dying hung to the nest -- glaring at me, refusing to let go. (Okay, the glaring part could be an exaggeration. But then again, maybe not).

I secured a long stick from her garage and -- after several tense moments -- knocked the nest to the ground.

I approached cautiously to see if there was any fight left in the wasps.

As I bent over to closely examine the nest, my vibrating watch alarm went off -- and I leaped off that porch with a leap that would make an Olympic High Jump Champion jealous.

Our friend was still laughing as I drove away. I am so proud that my leap of faith was not accompanied by girly-boy screams which almost escaped my lips.

And so it is, sometimes you have to face your fears (No, it doesn't have to be high noon) because it's the right thing to do. And often humor shows up during or after the experience to make it even more memorable.

Now pause and breathe in ... breathe out, with a HINT of a smile. WOW. Looks GOOD on you. Y-E-A-H.

FUNOMENAL™ Positivity Best Practice: TODAY, I invite you to face a fear that is stopping you from being all you can be. You know the one.

How do you face a fear? You can do it by using my favorite acronym for F.E.A.R. -- Finding Excuses and Reasons.

If you find enough excuses you won't face any fear, and you will never be all you can be. But if you find just one BIG enough reason to face it, you'll not only face it -- you'll overcome it.

Is your fear based on real evidence or an imagined scenario? Either way, ask, "What happens if I don't face this and overcome it? What's possible if I do? How can I use humor to help me? Who can help me?"

Act immediately on any impressions that feel right. You can do this. Now, go deal with that bad-boy F.E.A.R. TODAY.

Be FUNOMENAL™: have more fun, get more done, and bring out the best in everyone. You can do this.

"All you need to face and overcome a fear is to find a bigger reason for doing it than for not doing it. You can do this." - Tony Brigmon

FUNOMENAL™ Nuggets of Positivity (at a glance)

- Be FUNOMENAL™
- Share the love
- Get serious about FUN
- Use your gift to help others
- Do what you look forward to
- Listen to others to energize
- Give unexpected meaningful gifts

- Smile to energize
- Turn dumb do's into smart success
- Lead or follow the leader
- Focus on what people care about
- Use their name and remember their interest
- Lift others to lift self
- Use M.U.S.I.C. to energize-engage-enrich
  - Motivate
  - Unwind
  - Smile
  - I Love Ya
  - Communicate

- Give what they want to have all you want
- Get results with accountability
- Do what you value for energy
- Create the dream to attract the team
- Share smile stories
- Decide with Bubble Up -- Bubble Down
- Do what you love and do best

- Ask others for their success formula
- Use fun to build trust
- Wish others well
- Preview success
- View the next ONE thing
- Review to improve

- Do what you were made to do
- Communicate what you want

- Use the carrot and stick to motivate
- Do what the owner would do
- Use YOUR stories to communicate
- Set the tone for participation in 15 seconds
- Let the kid in you out to play to boost creativity
- Treat everyone as special
- Do private acts of kindness

- Get prepared, not scared
- Do what works for you for success
- Learn from every failure to succeed
- Use "I AM" for the WOW of NOW
- Use Yin-Yang energy to succeed
- Find a GOOD reason to overcome your fear
- Begin with the MAIN THANG

Smile &
Wave
Make someone's day!

"S.M.I.L.E. Positivity Best Practices"

To help you capture and remember the positives in your life, the "S.M.I.L.E. Positivity Best Practices" are fast, simple, and effective. Each one of the five steps is research-proven to boost happiness.

If you've tried the practice of journaling before, had every intention of keeping up with it, but inevitably fell short, the "S.M.I.L.E. Positivity Best Practices" are for you. The science behind these journal entries -- putting your brain in a positive state -- is solid.

This journal is different. It's guided. And it focuses on the key areas of our lives that we should be thinking about if we want to maximize our experiences and live our life to the fullest.

The guided areas of writing are based on research in the field of positive psychology. They will make a notable difference in how you see the world, what you choose to focus on, and most importantly, how you talk and react to those you care the most about.

According to Dr. Rick Hanson, a neuropsychologist, a member of U.C. Berkeley's Greater Good Science Center's advisory board, and author of the book *Hardwiring Happiness: The New Brain Science of Contentment, Calm, and Confidence*, our brains are naturally wired to focus on the negative, which can make us feel stressed and unhappy even though there are a lot of positive things in our lives.

He says, "Taking in the good (positive things) around you usually takes less than half a minute. Any single time you do this won't change your life. But half a dozen times a day, day after day, you really can gradually change your brain from the inside out."

The "S.M.I.L.E. Positivity Best Practices" are a great way for you to "take in the good" around you -- to put your brain in a positive state at the start and end of each day.

It's fast (less than 30 seconds for each entry): three steps in the morning and two at night.

The goal is to do at least six (there's three possible entries in step one). This gives you the daily half dozen positives Dr. Hanson recommends you "take in" to change your brain to focus on positives.

Yes, you can capture more than six positives if you wish. I do -- because it feels good.

Here's your "S.M.I.L.E. Positivity Best Practices" template. Have more fun. Get more done. Bring out the best in everyone.

S.M.I.L.E. Positivity Best Practices

(Put Your Brain in a State of Positive with S.M.I.L.E. Questions)

FUNomenal™ Goal: Record a Minimum of Six Positives a Day.

➢ **S - SMILE AND WAVE.**
  ○ Gratitude: Name three things you have that you would miss if you no longer had them and why. Say, "Thank You" after each one.
  ○ Think of something that made you smile or laugh out loud.
  ○ Think of something you are looking forward to. Calendar it if applicable.
➢ **M - Make Their Day.**
  ○ Ask, "Who can I help, praise, congratulate, wish well, or thank?" Notice what name comes to mind.
  ○ Pay them a visit, give them a call, text them, email them, or send them a handwritten note.
➢ **I - It Would Be Great If ... What?**
  ○ What would be GREAT? (Yes, you can have FUN with this!)
  ○ Name three outcomes you want today. (Example: I got started. I kept going. It all worked out.)

- Envision what you want as already true. Then, say, "Thank You" for what is already yours in the future.
➤ **L - Look for the Good. Share it.**
  - If you are with someone, ask yourself, "What's good about her or him?" Share the good you see in them.
  - What is good in your life right now?
  - What was GOOD about today?
➤ **E - Easy Does It. Be Here. NOW. Paying Attention.**
  - There is only ONE thing to do. The next ONE thing.
  - Where am I? (Here)
  - What am I doing? (This)
  - Describe it: "I am …."

~~~

Smile & Wave

Make someone's day!

"Good Notes to Self" Workbook

"Good Notes to Self" is the letter "L" (LOOK FOR THE GOOD — SHARE IT) on the "S.M.I.L.E. Positivity Best Practices." It's the best way I know to be your own best friend because it rewires your brain to look first for the good every day in every way in everything.

By capturing the good in writing you can revisit it anytime you wish for a positive energy boost and even share it with others for their good.

So, if you choose not to do all 5 steps of the daily S.M.I.L.E. Positivity Best Practices (but I encourage you to), then I highly recommend that you do at least Step 4, by using this "Good Notes to Self" Workbook.

Think about some good things you learned today -- from your own experience or from someone else's experience. Shoot to capture a half-dozen "Good Notes to Self" for future use. Looking for the good puts your brain in a positive state and over time it will rewire your brain to look first for positives in all situations.

Looking for the good begins with this question, "What's good?" Here are a couple of good things that came into my mind when I asked the question.

> It's GOOD to look for the good -- BECAUSE that's how you find it. And when you find good, it energizes your body, mind, and spirit – which motivates you to look for more good. So, what's good?

> It's GOOD to lead side-by-side rather than from the front -- BECAUSE there are more on your side that way, and your back is harder to be hit by 'friendly' fire.

Because recent research now shows "66" days seems to be the magic number of days on average before a new behavior becomes automatic (not 21 days), we'll go with that number here in the "Good Notes to Self" Workbook.

And I'll be here with you every day sharing my "Good Notes to Self" as well. In fact, I've already made the 66-day trip and have my "Good Notes to Self" waiting for you now, with the hope you may benefit from some of mine too.

I'll share my three "Good Notes to Self" with you each day, and there's room for you to capture at least three of your own.

Your "Good Notes to Self" will serve as a priceless review of good things Life taught you. This is why it's important to write them down. Reviewing them will help you to remember to keep your brain in a state of positive, so you can deal effectively with the negatives.

And when the time is right, and those you care about are receptive, you can share some of your "Good Notes to Self" for their benefit too.

You'll notice some of your "Good Notes to Self" will include Life lessons you learn from your "teachers." Who are your teachers? Actually, everyone. You can silently thank those who teach you what NOT to do (because that's good too), and openly thank those who teach you something that would be good for you to do.

Remember, all life lessons -- from both good and not-so-good experiences -- put your brain in a state of positive, which makes you more productive, persuasive, faster, and more accurate. So, it's ALL good? It's ALL good.

If you're like me, you may want to capture your "Good Notes to Self" electronically rather than here in the workbook section. I like to capture mine as part of my "S.M.I.L.E. Positivity Best Practices" on my Google Calendar where they are easily accessible.

So if you record your "Good Notes to Self" elsewhere like me, you can just put a check mark ("✓") after each 1-2-3 in the workbook -- remembering, of course, to say DONE! after each one.

A great leader was once asked his success formula for inspiring legendary productivity from his followers. His response was simple and powerful, "I teach them correct principles and let them govern themselves." Wow. You can do this too.

You can use **your** "Good Notes to Self" as well as mine, if you'd like, to teach correct principles to your workplace team -- and even share them with family and friends.

Let's get started now with your "Good Notes to Self".

Think about your day today, including what went well and what didn't go so well. There's a Life Lesson in each one waiting for you to capture it. Do it here in this workbook section or on an electronic device.

Doing this will put your brain in a state of positive so you can be at your best.

First, my "Good Notes to Self" for your review. Then, after my three you can add yours here (or elsewhere). If you add them elsewhere, remember to put a "✓" after each of the three numbers here, followed by an out-loud fun DONE! You can do this. So -- YNOT?

"Good Notes to Self": Day 1

My Notes:
If you aim to selflessly serve rather than people-please, your aim will be better served and more people will be pleased.

Spending 5-minutes in the presence of those who love you can heal hours of stress from being in the presence of those who don't.

End your relationship with Perfection and have an affair with Good Enough. Good Enough can feel like ... well ... perfect.

Your Notes:

Be FUNOMENAL™: have more fun, get more done, and bring out the best in everyone.

"Good Notes to Self": Day 2

My Notes:
Don't be swayed by negative people. They have a problem with EVERY solution. It's a toxic negative pollution. They're miserable.

When your prince charming gets lost and is too stubborn to ask for directions, smile. This is PROOF he needs you.

Say 'DONE!' out loud when you complete a To-Do. And notice what 'DONE!' does for you. And to procrastination too. Woo hoo.

Your Notes:

Be FUNOMENAL™: have more fun, get more done, and bring out the best in everyone.

"Good Notes to Self": Day 3

My Notes:
Pay attention to gut feelings. They can help you know when to start, stop, and continue. Want a Life? Listen to your gut. NOW.

Bad judgment ends in pain. If it didn't, you wouldn't be motivated to upgrade to better judgment. Thank you, Pain. Got it.

'Let me help you with that' beats 'May I help you?' It sounds more like you really mean it. And the help you give will help you.

Your Notes:

Be FUNOMENAL™: have more fun, get more done, and bring out the best in everyone.

"Good Notes to Self": Day 4

My Notes:
Action, not good intentions, makes things better. Time to escalate some good intentions to action? Better.

To be the best YOU is what you're here to do, not to be the best copycat. Copy that? Good.

Ask yourself, 'What advice do you have for me today?'. Act on the internal answer. Say, 'Thank you.'

Your Notes:

Be FUNOMENAL™: have more fun, get more done, and bring out the best in everyone.

"Good Notes to Self": Day 5

My Notes:
Sometimes you must burn a bridge to light the way to a better day. To see best, don't look back.

It's the simple things that make you happy, not the complicated. Not happy? You've complicated something. Back to simple.

Surround yourself with people who also have dreams. Yours and theirs will cheer each other on. And the surround sound ROCKS.

Your Notes:

Be FUNOMENAL™: have more fun, get more done, and bring out the best in everyone.

"Good Notes to Self": Day 6

My Notes:
DO NOT use Facebook to dish dirt on others. It drains those who read it and defaces you. Face it.

Someday is NOT one of the seven days of the week. But it makes a week weak. Nothing good happens someday. Only today. Do it.

If happiness is what happiness does, what is unhappiness? Same answer. Do happy. Be happy.

Your Notes:

Be FUNOMENAL™: have more fun, get more done, and bring out the best in everyone.

"Good Notes to Self": Day 7

My Notes:
Saying 'Something wonderful is about to happen!' opens your eyes to wonderful things that ARE happening. Hello, Wonderful.

Being grateful for what you HAVE invites what you WANT to show up at the gratitude party too. When it does, say, 'Thank You.'

Before you can enjoy it all, you have to work and pay for it all. The FULL perk of the joy part is worth the other parts. Do it.

Your Notes:

Be FUNOMENAL™: have more fun, get more done, and bring out the best in everyone.

"Good Notes to Self": Day 8

My Notes:
Begin at the end. It's the only way to know if the trip from the beginning will be worth it.

When you do what it takes to make someone happy, Happy does what it takes to make you even happier. Can you take it?

When you say and mean, "Let's make something good happen!", what happens? Something GOOD. Say it. Mean it.

Your Notes:

Be FUNOMENAL™: have more fun, get more done, and bring out the best in everyone.

"Good Notes to Self": Day 9

My Notes:
When you stand up for someone who is down, it puts both of you on higher ground. Stand up. Lift up.

If you don't make a macro out of a micro, you'll handle the micro better. You can MACRO this.

Jets don't have rear-view mirrors. They were made to go forward. So were you. Go forward. Enjoy the view.

Your Notes:

Be FUNOMENAL™: have more fun, get more done, and bring out the best in everyone.

"Good Notes to Self": Day 10

My Notes:
When you come back to NOW, you exit the sad past or anxious future, which do not exist here. Don't let them rob your NOW.

Remember how blessed you are. It helps you forget how stressed you were.

When you learn from a battle you lost, you didn't lose. You won.

Your Notes:

Be FUNOMENAL™: have more fun, get more done, and bring out the best in everyone.

"Good Notes to Self": Day 11

My Notes:
Thank God for everything and ask for little. That's when He biggie-sizes the littles.

Tears say what you can't in a prayer. If they show up, let them speak. They get a TOP Priority Response from the MAN upstairs.

What you focus on expands. Focus on the positives. You can find positives in negatives if you look for them. Look.

Your Notes:

Be FUNOMENAL™: have more fun, get more done, and bring out the best in everyone.

"Good Notes to Self": Day 12

My Notes:

A bruise means you were there, but you won't remember it. A scar means 'there' taught you something to remember.

Look for the good in others. It improves your looks in their eyes. Have a good look. Today.

The greater the storm, the brighter the rainbow. Look UP to weather the storm and bask in the rainbow.

Your Notes:

Be FUNOMENAL™: have more fun, get more done, and bring out the best in everyone.

"Good Notes to Self": Day 13

My Notes:
Sharing with someone a beautiful quality you see in them expands that beautiful quality within you. Go ahead. Share.

Don't quit. Let go. Quitting drains your GO battery. Letting go charges it for moving on to better. Let go. Move on. Today.

Doing small things with great love is no small thing. It's the best way to make a small good thing a BIGGIE.

Your Notes:

Be FUNOMENAL™: have more fun, get more done, and bring out the best in everyone.

"Good Notes to Self": Day 14

My Notes:
Admitting to each other the pain you caused each other beats hurting each other for the pain the other caused you. Heal the pain.

People don't stand up at funerals and say, 'She had a really expensive couch and great shoes.' They say, 'She was there for me.'

Spending time with those you love, doing something they love, expands the love.

Your Notes:

Be FUNOMENAL™: have more fun, get more done, and bring out the best in everyone.

"Good Notes to Self": Day 15

My Notes:
Stretching to reach something you really want expands your reach.

Take the time to discover, develop, and distribute your gifts to help others. It feels great and inspires them to do the same.

Bumps on the road of life are there to slow you down so gratitude can catch up to appreciate the smooth stretches ahead.

Your Notes:

Be FUNOMENAL™: have more fun, get more done, and bring out the best in everyone.

"Good Notes to Self": Day 16

My Notes:
Point your camera at better scenes to get better pictures. This is not about cameras or pictures. Just better points.

Play the role you play best for the team's success. This inspires the team to add their best for OUR success.

It's not naive to be positive. It's smart and courageous. The improved situation will thank and salute you.

Your Notes:

Be FUNOMENAL™: have more fun, get more done, and bring out the best in everyone.

"Good Notes to Self": Day 17

My Notes:
Be kind to unkind people. The least kindness or unkindness makes the universe respond in kind to you.

Believe good can come from negatives. It can inspire you to take another shot at the positives. Camera. Ready. Action.

When a police officer pulls you over and says, 'Papers,' is not the time to say, 'Scissors.' It could increase the papers.

Your Notes:

Be FUNOMENAL™: have more fun, get more done, and bring out the best in everyone.

"Good Notes to Self": Day 18

My Notes:
Do good. If someone says something bad about you, the good people won't believe it. What the others believe doesn't matter.

Just because vulgar words rhyme doesn't mean they deserve to be listened to. Vulgar words degrade. Right words inspire. Right on.

You don't have to give those who are ALWAYS angry and complaining your time. Your time deserves better vibes than that.

Your Notes:

Be FUNOMENAL™: have more fun, get more done, and bring out the best in everyone.

"Good Notes to Self": Day 19

My Notes:
Asking, 'What would be great today for us to do together?' inspires great experiences together. Great awaits. Ask the question.

It's GOOD to NOT be alright with something that's ALL wrong. All wrong never leads to feeling alright.

Life's not about who you used to be. It's about who you've become. If you find that unbecoming, become better. Today.

Your Notes:

Be FUNOMENAL™: have more fun, get more done, and bring out the best in everyone.

"Good Notes to Self": Day 20

My Notes:
The place where you don't have to prove yourself to anybody is inside you. You can take that place anywhere.

Saying to your ONE and only, 'I'd choose you in a hundred worlds and lifetimes' increases the chances they'd choose you too.

The past is not a good place to live, but it's a great place to grow from. You can take the lessons with you without the drama.

Your Notes:

Be FUNOMENAL™: have more fun, get more done, and bring out the best in everyone.

"Good Notes to Self": Day 21

My Notes:
The best treatment is to treat others as real friends. When you need treatment, real friends will show up with treats for you.

When that voice in your head, pretending to be you, says you're not good enough, tell it, 'Liar, liar, pants on fire! I am!'

If you undervalue who you are and overvalue who you're not, your value is shot. Value who you are and the good you can do.

Your Notes:

Be FUNOMENAL™: have more fun, get more done, and bring out the best in everyone.

"Good Notes to Self": Day 22

My Notes:
Hope's favorite place to appear is in the stillness of heartfelt prayer. Keep going there.

Do the right thing, especially when nobody's watching. It turns on your heart light, which people can't resist admiring.

Be friendly first. The chain-reaction of friendly beats the chainsaw reaction of unfriendly. Friendly ways make better days.

Your Notes:

Be FUNOMENAL™: have more fun, get more done, and bring out the best in everyone.

"Good Notes to Self": Day 23

My Notes:
If the town is too small for the dream in your head, leave. The greatest thing you can do for that town is to succeed. Do it.

If you're lost and you feel calm, you're not lost. Follow your inner GPS. This is not just about how to get to an address.

Look in the mirror and ask, 'What do I need to change to succeed?' This check-up from the neck-up can inspire positive change.

Your Notes:

Be FUNOMENAL™: have more fun, get more done, and bring out the best in everyone.

"Good Notes to Self": Day 24

My Notes:
Distance yourself from negativity. That's when the shortcut to positivity appears. Go the distance for the positives.

You know more than they think, think more than you speak, and notice more than they realize. You should not be underestimated.

Smile silently when someone expects you to be enraged. It's one of the coolest things you can do for rage, for you, and for them.

Your Notes:

Be FUNOMENAL™: have more fun, get more done, and bring out the best in everyone.

"Good Notes to Self": Day 25

My Notes:
Admit it when you're wrong and be quiet when you're right. This makes them forget the wrong and remember the right. Right on.

DUMB means you didn't think it through. STUPID means you did it more than once. Think. Don't be STUPID.

Be grateful for little things. It attracts BIGGER things to be grateful for. Ingratitude destroys everything. Boo that.

Your Notes:

Be FUNOMENAL™: have more fun, get more done, and bring out the best in everyone.

"Good Notes to Self": Day 26

My Notes:
Touch your planner before you touch your phone. This makes your phone your friend and not a waste of productive time, AGAIN.

Saying NO to what's NOT important empowers you to say YES to what is. NO? YES.

Look for little ways to be a better person. Little ways make room for better days.

Your Notes:

Be FUNOMENAL™: have more fun, get more done, and bring out the best in everyone.

"Good Notes to Self": Day 27

My Notes:
How would it feel if this were already DONE? Great? Begin within 5-seconds and you've won -- the fight with procrastination.

The effort to make yourself miserable or happy is about the same. Hint: the return on happy is WAY better. Go HAPPY.

Sharing what it was like after you crossed the bridge of your insecurities makes the insecurities of others jump off the bridge.

Your Notes:

Be FUNOMENAL™: have more fun, get more done, and bring out the best in everyone.

"Good Notes to Self": Day 28

My Notes:
When someone reacts to your quirks with 'Me too', you have a new friend. Do you hum in the shower? Me too.

Let friendly silence speak for you at times. It can draw things out of others that you may need to hear.

A lack of boundaries invites a lack of respect. Respectfully set them. Most will respect this. Say goodbye to those who won't.

Your Notes:

Be FUNOMENAL™: have more fun, get more done, and bring out the best in everyone.

"Good Notes to Self": Day 29

My Notes:
Replace 'Why me?' with 'How can I?' and 'How can we?' You get better answers and better solutions.

Strength comes AFTER you've been weak, fearless AFTER you've been afraid, and wisdom AFTER you've been foolish. Keep going.

Bake, make or buy a favorite food for someone you love. It'll make their day and yours. Make it, bake it, or buy it. Try it.

Your Notes:

Be FUNOMENAL™: have more fun, get more done, and bring out the best in everyone.

"Good Notes to Self": Day 30

My Notes:
Ask 'What would be GREAT today?' GREAT answers to that question empower Possibility. You'll be amazed at what's possible.

Bring your attention back to what you're doing NOW because NOW is where Calm, Contentment, and Inspiration live.

When you finally believe you ARE good enough, you begin to do more and receive more than enough. Believe it!

Your Notes:

Be FUNOMENAL™: have more fun, get more done, and bring out the best in everyone.

"Good Notes to Self": Day 31

My Notes:
Fill someone's cup in some 'cool' (good) way and you become a warm cup of WONDERFUL, which makes everyone's day.

Learn something new. Share what you learned. That's when information escalates to knowledge.

The tears that sneak out of your eyes and roll down your cheeks are the ones that heal. Let them do their job.

Your Notes:

Be FUNOMENAL™: have more fun, get more done, and bring out the best in everyone.

"Good Notes to Self": Day 32

My Notes:
Not every life that looks good on the outside feels good on the inside. Improve your life from the inside out.

Stay positive and work hard. Staying negative and not working hard makes everything harder. Am I sure? Positive.

When the phone rings, let it be your reminder to smile. A smile can be felt over the phone. Ring. Ring. Smile.

Your Notes:

Be FUNOMENAL™: have more fun, get more done, and bring out the best in everyone.

"Good Notes to Self": Day 33

My Notes:
Saying, 'Here goes nothing' at the start of something, keeps nothing from stopping you from giving it your best something.

The best form of pretty is to be pretty kind, pretty funny, pretty smart, and pretty strong. And that is irresistibly attractive.

To listen to what someone has to say is the sincerest form of respect. It boomerangs back to you. Listen up. For respect.

Your Notes:

Be FUNOMENAL™: have more fun, get more done, and bring out the best in everyone.

"Good Notes to Self": Day 34

My Notes:
Take a nap when you're feeling negative. It gives positives the chance to wake up and shut up the negatives.

Believe good will come out of a struggle. It helps you look for the good and stop dwelling on the struggle. Believe it.

The end of a bad relationship reveals what you were too blinded by love to see in the beginning. The end. No, wait. The beginning.

Your Notes:

Be FUNOMENAL™: have more fun, get more done, and bring out the best in everyone.

"Good Notes to Self": Day 35

My Notes:
Before you can reach the Land of Sure, you have to navigate the Waters of Unsure. Am I sure? Yep. Keep paddling.

Stress says, "I want it NOW." Faith says, "If it's right, I'll get it when it's right. Faith is right. Believe it.

When you let a bad experience teach you, it heals the pain of what hurt you. Look for the lesson. Move past the pain.

Your Notes:

Be FUNOMENAL™: have more fun, get more done, and bring out the best in everyone.

"Good Notes to Self": Day 36

My Notes:
Look for the 'gold' in others. You get a better return than looking for the dirt. Go for the gold. Ditch the dirt.

Sometimes it's not what's wrong with you that troubles a few, it's what's right. Don't let a skewed view stop the good you do.

When you decide to do something, no matter what, obstacles aren't BIG enough to stop YOU. Decide. Do it. No matter what. Today.

Your Notes:

Be FUNOMENAL™: have more fun, get more done, and bring out the best in everyone.

"Good Notes to Self": Day 37

My Notes:

You teach people how to treat you by what you allow. Make it clear what you do and don't allow. The treats will improve.

Really mean what you say. If you don't really mean it, they won't believe what you said. Believe it. Say it. Mean it.

If someone feels alone when you're with them, you're not in a relationship with them. You're in one with you. You have Work to do.

Your Notes:

Be FUNOMENAL™: have more fun, get more done, and bring out the best in everyone.

"Good Notes to Self": Day 38

My Notes:
When you meet someone and your soul says, 'There you are, I've been looking for you', you found the ONE. Now be their ONE.

Pour everything you have into what you love and you'll never be empty. Do what you love for those you love. Fill 'er up.

Smile at Life and it smiles back at you. Laugh at Life and you get the best laugh. True.

Your Notes:

Be FUNOMENAL™: have more fun, get more done, and bring out the best in everyone.

"Good Notes to Self": Day 39

My Notes:
To refrain from responding with sarcasm within seconds of a stupid question is a sign of brilliance. Forget the stupid signs.

Listen to that still, small voice within you. It will tell you where to go, what to do, and what to say. Yea!

You can only live in the NOW. Dwelling on the depressing/angry past or anxious future is NOT living. It's suffering.

Your Notes:

Be FUNOMENAL™: have more fun, get more done, and bring out the best in everyone.

"Good Notes to Self": Day 40

My Notes:
The shortest path to a happy ending is an honest beginning of how it really is now and how you want it to be.

Choose CALM to access CALM power. Your alive-and-well peaceful remains will thank you. Power up!

Everything is 'figureoutable'. You're able. Take time out. Figure. Now play it forward. See? No doubtable, it's figureoutable.

Your Notes:

Be FUNOMENAL™: have more fun, get more done, and bring out the best in everyone.

"Good Notes to Self": Day 41

My Notes:
The struggle you're in today gives you the strength you'll need tomorrow. Having fun today? Same thing.

An original is worth more than a copy. YOU are original. Copy that? Good.

To silently wish others, 'May you be well. May you be happy. May you have more than enough.' attracts the GOOD stuff to you.

Your Notes:

Be FUNOMENAL™: have more fun, get more done, and bring out the best in everyone.

"Good Notes to Self": Day 42

My Notes:
'If it went right, how would it go?' is a powerful question to help things grow. It attracts GROW ideas. Act on them.

Sharing the good you see in others opens their eyes to the good in you and to the good all around them. It's ALL good.

Dwell on the positives in your life. Dwelling on the negatives is a miserable dwelling. What's good in your life?

Your Notes:

Be FUNOMENAL™: have more fun, get more done, and bring out the best in everyone.

"Good Notes to Self": Day 43

My Notes:
When someone opens up to you, they think you're pretty special. And you have a special responsibility to honor their trust.

Write a new chapter in your life. Make it a better read than the old one you don't want to be read out loud. Write? Right.

When you re-frame a problem as an opportunity, it's more fun to look at and easier to resolve. Happy opportunities to you today.

Your Notes:

Be FUNOMENAL™: have more fun, get more done, and bring out the best in everyone.

"Good Notes to Self": Day 44

My Notes:
Care more about what YOU think of you than what others think. You'll cease to be their prisoner. Hello FREEDOM.

STRESS is your 'check engine' warning light. To ignore it or hope it'll go away is a bad idea. Check. Change something.

Imagine the one who cuts you off in traffic is rushing to the hospital. Any thoughts harsher than that can put you in one.

Your Notes:

Be FUNOMENAL™: have more fun, get more done, and bring out the best in everyone.

"Good Notes to Self": Day 45

My Notes:
Practice gratitude every day. Those who do, tend to have more birthdays. And they live happier longer.

Try, 'Please don't take it personally when I tell you NO. I'm using it on everyone right now. I'm in YES recovery.' It works.

Following up 'Can you? with 'Will you?' helps. People tend to do what they commit to, not what they CAN do.

Your Notes:

Be FUNOMENAL™: have more fun, get more done, and bring out the best in everyone.

"Good Notes to Self": Day 46

My Notes:
If you do it when convenient, it's an interest. If you HAVE to do it, no matter what, it matters. What really matters?

How to have the best day of your life: give life your best. Yes, you can have a LOT of best days. Make today one of them.

WHO you have in your life matters more than WHAT you have. Time with WHAT, at the expense of WHO, is too expensive.

Your Notes:

Be FUNOMENAL™: have more fun, get more done, and bring out the best in everyone.

"Good Notes to Self": Day 47

My Notes:
Hitting rock bottom gives you a firm foundation for a better life. Now get off your bottom and build it with what you've learned.

Accept the truth. STOP the nonsense of trying to convince your head what your heart knows is a lie. Hello FREEDOM.

To get out of your chair and do something thoughtful for someone is the best way to save a seat in their future.

Your Notes:

Be FUNOMENAL™: have more fun, get more done, and bring out the best in everyone.

"Good Notes to Self": Day 48

My Notes:
You create your own heartbreak with expectation. You mend it with appreciation of what you already have.

Life takes a turn for better when you stop looking around for the remote. Get up and make the change to a better station.

Who would you tell first if something amazing happened to you? This is your best friend. They're amazing too. Tell them.

Your Notes:

Be FUNOMENAL™: have more fun, get more done, and bring out the best in everyone.

"Good Notes to Self": Day 49

My Notes:
20 seconds of 'insane courage' is all it takes to launch something great. Got 20 seconds? Insane courage? Great. Launch.

When you walk into a room and think 'Why am I here?', the answer won't budge till you walk out of the room. Walk to the answer.

What to do if you're a fruit loop in a world of Cheerios: cheerfully help them in every way you can. They'll cheer.

Your Notes:

Be FUNOMENAL™: have more fun, get more done, and bring out the best in everyone.

"Good Notes to Self": Day 50

My Notes:
Someone who wouldn't mind waking up with you, seeing you in wrinkles with gray hair is a keeper. Find 'em. Keep 'em.

Spreading positive vibes attract other positive vibes. Then they all get together and throw a surprise party for you.

Have a grateful heart. Anything you begin that way is going to end WAY better. Check in with your heart. Get ready. Start.

Your Notes:

Be FUNOMENAL™: have more fun, get more done, and bring out the best in everyone.

"Good Notes to Self": Day 51

My Notes:
The only thing standing between you and what you can REALLY do is the story you keep telling yourself. Time for a better story.

Make a U-turn when it doesn't feel right. Your inner GPS doesn't lie. Turn around. Dead ahead is deadly trouble.

There's a cure for 'Some-timers' (sometimes I remember and sometimes I don't). Write it down. Set an alarm. Do it.

Your Notes:

Be FUNOMENAL™: have more fun, get more done, and bring out the best in everyone.

"Good Notes to Self": Day 52

My Notes:
Life is NOT about wringing maximum miles out of your body, but about bringing maximum smiles to everybody. Bring it.

The FORCE can only be accessed by 'Oh, Be YOU'. Be yourself. The FORCE will be with you. It's true, Oh, Be YOU.

It's what you have that money can't buy that makes you truly rich. What do you have? Think about it.

Your Notes:

Be FUNOMENAL™: have more fun, get more done, and bring out the best in everyone.

"Good Notes to Self": Day 53

My Notes:

Pay attention to whatever inspires you. It's inviting you out to play. RSVP immediately. You may find it pays.

Happy? Yes? Keep doing what you're doing. No? Do you want to be happy? No? Keep doing what you're doing. Yes? Change something.

Contracts 101: the BIG print giveth and the small print taketh away. If the small takes more than the BIG gives, don't play.

Your Notes:

Be FUNOMENAL™: have more fun, get more done, and bring out the best in everyone.

"Good Notes to Self": Day 54

My Notes:
Music can be a safety net to catch you when you fall. Playing favorite oldies first can help you avoid the fall.

Eat like you love yourself and you'll eat better. You'll move, speak, and act better too. Show yourself some love. Eat better.

Stop comparing yourself to others. No one can be the best you but you. There's no comparison.

Your Notes:

Be FUNOMENAL™: have more fun, get more done, and bring out the best in everyone.

"Good Notes to Self": Day 55

My Notes:
Your greatest talent is more powerful than your biggest fear.
This is what fear is afraid of. Do your thing. No fear.

Write an angry letter, then throw it away. Research shows
what you throw away is anger's power over you. Write it. Toss
it.

The way people treat you is a statement of who THEY are.
The way you respond, a statement of who you are. Make a
better statement.

Your Notes:

Be FUNOMENAL™: have more fun, get more done, and
bring out the best in everyone.

"Good Notes to Self": Day 56

My Notes:
It pays to be humble. If you're wrong, there's no fall off a high horse. When you're right, they love you for not getting on one.

Do what you love to do and were meant to do. Anything less than that can't do as much for you.

Be nice to someone you want to throw a brick at. It will soften the brick they want to throw at you.

Your Notes:

Be FUNOMENAL™: have more fun, get more done, and bring out the best in everyone.

"Good Notes to Self": Day 57

My Notes:
A woman's hands and arms speak volumes. Hands around your throat: you'd better listen! Arms around your neck: you did!

There are perks from going through a bad experience. You discover who cares about you. You gain a new appreciation for good.

If you can't control what's happening, you CAN control how you respond. That's where your power is and what they'll remember.

Your Notes:

Be FUNOMENAL™: have more fun, get more done, and bring out the best in everyone.

"Good Notes to Self": Day 58

My Notes:
There's no such thing as a little lie. Once discovered, it turns a fire hose of doubt on every other truth expressed.

Just because you share a proven way doesn't mean they are going to do it, till the pain of not doing it talks them into it.

Reducing negatives does not produce positives. But if you look for positives, the negatives can't reproduce. Yes, I'm positive.

Your Notes:

Be FUNOMENAL™: have more fun, get more done, and bring out the best in everyone.

"Good Notes to Self": Day 59

My Notes:
The magnitude of the blessing coming exceeds that of the battle you're facing. Fight a good fight. Enjoy the blessing.

The antidote for a tragic flair for failure is a YES to the magic dare of doing what makes you feel most alive.

Much of what weighs you down is not yours to carry. Put down the part that's not yours. Better? Carry on.

Your Notes:

Be FUNOMENAL™: have more fun, get more done, and bring out the best in everyone.

"Good Notes to Self": Day 60

My Notes:
Effort can do more for you now than perfection. Keep trying?
Perfect.

Usually, the one who needs to get out of your way is YOU,
the negative you. Tell that bad boy, 'Get out of my way!'
Today.

Look forward. It's the best way to stop stumbling over what's
behind you. You can do this. Ready? Look. Move. Forward.

Your Notes:

Be FUNOMENAL™: have more fun, get more done, and
bring out the best in everyone.

"Good Notes to Self": Day 61

My Notes:
Treat people in a way they'll miss. When they miss you, they'll call. If you miss them, call them.

Stay close to your family. In the blink of an eye, a man stands where a boy was and a woman where a girl was. It's worth it.

At any moment, you have the power to say, 'This is NOT how the story is going to end!' To be continued ... by you.

Your Notes:

Be FUNOMENAL™: have more fun, get more done, and bring out the best in everyone.

"Good Notes to Self": Day 62

My Notes:
Take the time to do the right thing right. If you don't, it's an insult to Time AND the Right Thing. Right on.

Count YOUR blessings. Stop counting THEIR flaws. The sum total of your blessings reduces the 'bum' total of their flaws.

Sometimes you fall down because there's something down there you're supposed to find. Look for the good. Find it when you fall.

Your Notes:

Be FUNOMENAL™: have more fun, get more done, and bring out the best in everyone.

"Good Notes to Self": Day 63

My Notes:
It's okay to cheat on Fear, break up with Doubt, and move in with a good Dream and walk away from a bad one.

Doubt says, 'Impossible.' Fear says, 'Too risky.' Reason says, 'Pointless.' Faith says, 'We can do this!' Believe it.

Taste the words before you send them out. If the taste is bitter, spit them out -- of your head, not your mouth.

Your Notes:

Be FUNOMENAL™: have more fun, get more done, and bring out the best in everyone.

"Good Notes to Self": Day 64

My Notes:
Negative thoughts aren't the problem. They just show up. The problems begin when you invite them to stay for some drama.

A weak man can't love a strong woman. True love makes weak men strong. And strong women can't resist true love. Man up.

When you walk with someone through a difficult time, you'll never have to worry about where you stand with that person.

Your Notes:

Be FUNOMENAL™: have more fun, get more done, and bring out the best in everyone.

"Good Notes to Self": Day 65

My Notes:
You get a better return throwing compliments like confetti than remarks that cut like a machete. Make it a nice throw.

If you try and fail and don't fail to keep trying, you don't fail. You are closer to success. Wow. Keep trying.

Look for a WAY rather than an EXCUSE. A WAY will take you to YOUR dream. An EXCUSE will keep you in your nightmare. Find a WAY.

Your Notes:

Be FUNOMENAL™: have more fun, get more done, and bring out the best in everyone.

"Good Notes to Self": Day 66

My Notes:
Put that thought on paper before it's lost in vapor. What's in your head, you will lose. What's in writing, you can use.

If you work at a job where you don't feel or show compassion, you're not at work. You're at war.

If you keep your eyes on the goal, the obstacles can't stare you down. And the goal will show you the workaround. Stay focused.

Your Notes:

Be FUNOMENAL™: have more fun, get more done, and bring out the best in everyone.

The MAIN THANG

Many years ago, at a small town Chamber of Commerce banquet in East Texas where I was the keynote speaker, I was seated at the head table next to a fun elderly gentleman.

Just before I was introduced to speak, he leaned over and said to me, "Would you like to hear something really PROfound?"

It's not every day I get asked an intriguing question like this by such a fascinating person, so I smiled and said, "Yes, I would." He said, "Brace yourself." I laughed and said, "I'm braced."

He said, "The MAIN thang is to keep the MAIN thang the MAIN thang -- and that's the MAIN thang." I laughed out-loud and vowed to never forget the MAIN thang.

What he said "stuck" with me and I began to share it with all of my audiences as a fun reminder to keep the MAIN thang the MAIN thang. I even have them repeat the whole line with me -- to their delight.

What my elderly friend shared with me was not only fun, it was indeed PROfound. What is the MAIN thang? It's your top priority -- the most important thing you need to get done TODAY.

DONE is FUN. To get the most important thing DONE gives you the best feeling AFTER it's done. Really.

And if you don't come up with a fun way to remind yourself daily of your top priority, other less important things can get in the way.

Research shows the most productive people ask daily "What is my top priority?" and write it down. But they don't stop there, they ask follow-up questions later in the day like, "Is what I wrote this morning still my top priority? Is what I'm doing right now line up with that?"

Now pause and breathe in ... breathe out, with a HINT of a smile. WOW. Looks GOOD on you. Y-E-A-H.

FUNOMENAL™ Positivity Best Practice: I invite you to begin asking yourself this FUNtastic question, the first thing in the morning, "What's the MAIN thang today -- my top priority?" Then begin the next step that takes you in that direction.

At noon, ask again, "What's the MAIN thang right now?" In the middle of the afternoon, repeat the question.

Sometimes the MAIN thang at the start of your day gets suddenly replaced by a bigger MAIN thang later in the day -- and you need to shift gears so you can keep your new MAIN thang the MAIN thang.

There's an old saying, "Life is what happens while you're making other plans." Asking yourself repeatedly the power question, "What's the MAIN thang right now? will help you keep the MAIN thang the MAIN "thing" -- even if the MAIN thang keeps changing.

The MAIN thang for me throughout this book has been to share with you LOTS of fun ways to keep your brain in a positive state, so you can be at your best to deal effectively with negativity and stress for greater productivity.

The world needs more **Funomenal™** people in it. You can be one. And guess what? Because you made it to **"The End"**, you have earned the right to BE one.

Are you ready? Brace yourself.

By the powers vested in me as

The original **Ambassador of FUN™**

I hereby declare

YOU

ARE

FUNOMENAL!

With all of the rights, privileges, and

responsibility to share

The FUNOMENAL™ WORKPLACE

Positivity

With everyone everywhere

CONGRATULATIONS!

Remember, no matter where you go -- there you are. So be there as **Funomenal™** YOU.

People will not only find you irresistibly attractive, but you will inspire increased productivity wherever you go. You can do this.

"The MAIN THANG is to keep the MAIN THANG the MAIN THANG and not let a DANG THANG keep you from the MAIN THANG." – Tony Brigmon

The End.

No wait – it's the beginning of the rest of your **Funomenal™** life.
To be continued …

*** To book Tony Brigmon as a keynote speaker to energize, entertain, and educate your audience -- or if you just want to share something fun, Tony would love to hear from you.
See TonyBrigmon.com

Made in the USA
Columbia, SC
23 August 2021